DAFT
PUNK

DAFT PUNK

A TRIP INSIDE
THE PYRAMID

DINA SANTORELLI

St. Martin's Press

NEW YORK

DAFT PUNK. Copyright © 2014 by Stonesong. All rights reserved. Printed in the United States of America. For information, address St. Martin's Press, 175 Fifth Avenue, New York, N.Y. 10010.

www.stmartins.com

Designed by Pyramid

The Library of Congress Cataloging-in-Publication Data is available upon request

ISBN 978-1-250-04997-1 (hardcover)

St. Martin's Press books may be purchased for educational, business, or promotional use. For information on bulk purchases, please contact Macmillan Corporate and Premium Sales Department at 1-800-221-7945, extension 5442, or write specialmarkets@macmillan.com.

First Edition: January 2014

10 9 8 7 6 5 4 3 2 1

CONTENTS

DAFT
PUNK

INTRODUCTION

Daft Punk is known to legions of music fans around the globe as the legendary and enigmatic French electronic dance music (EDM) duo consisting of Thomas Bangalter and Guy-Manuel de Homem-Christo. Affectionately dubbed "the robots" for their ever-present metallic helmets and gloves, Daft Punk has been on a groundbreaking musical voyage since the 1990s, meshing their love for EDM with their younger roots in pop, indie rock, and hip-hop. In the time since then, they have essentially revolutionized house music.

Although Daft Punk formed in the early 90s, their journey began the decade before in a small Paris bedroom where two adolescent boys, both fans of classic films and with similar and wide-ranging musical tastes (Bangalter once said, "There's no separation between what's hip and what's not"), formed a friendship. Together, they went on to make music that was personal and innovative, and to create a catalog that showcased their inclusive style, their knack for experimentation, and their curiosity about

technology. Over the course of twenty years, Daft Punk's body of work has blended music and mystique, and includes studio albums, live albums, compilation/remix albums, a soundtrack, music videos, films, collectibles, collaborations, commercials, revolutionary concert tours, and more. It's difficult to name other recording artists who have had their finger on the pulse of so many sounds and trends.

This book traces the extraordinary career of Daft Punk—from the bands, artists, and films that have influenced their music to their rise to international superstardom—and reveals the story of the men behind the masks. Daft Punk managed to not only achieve pop culture icon status, but also music industry respect. Anyone who's attended an electronic music show in recent years will find traces of the dynamic duo both in the program and the presentation, as many of today's artists feature Daft Punk's tracks, or samples of tracks, prominently on set lists and tap into the duo's groundbreaking live show format.

THE EARLY YEARS

THOMAS BANGALTER

Born in Paris, France, on January 3, 1975, Thomas Bangalter began playing the piano at the age of six (although he has said he was "forced" to play, he's now grateful to his parents for the push). Thomas's father, Daniel Vangarde (born Daniel Bangalter), is a French songwriter who penned and produced the 1970s hit song "D.I.S.C.O." by the French band Ottawan and "Cuba" by the Gibson Brothers, also based in France.

For his ninth or tenth birthday, Bangalter remembers having a small party in his bedroom—the room that would one day become Daft Punk's home studio, where they recorded their first two albums, *Homework* and *Discovery.* At the time, however, it was simply a dance floor where girls and boys partied to the grooves on the Giorgio Moroder–scored *Flashdance* soundtrack.

The Year Thomas Bangalter Was Born

▸ Singer Donna Summer releases the song "Love to Love You Baby," produced by Giorgio Moroder.

▸ The film version of The Who's *Tommy* premieres in London.

▸ *Saturday Night Live* makes its debut on network television.

▸ *The Rocky Horror Picture Show* premieres in theaters (although the film bombs, it goes on to generate a massive underground following, making it the longest-running theatrical release in film history).

▸ Popular films include *Jaws, The Towering Inferno, Benji, Young Frankenstein, Funny Lady, The Return of the Pink Panther,* and *One Flew Over the Cuckoo's Nest.*

▸ Jefferson Starship, KISS, Led Zeppelin, John Lennon, Pink Floyd, Bob Marley and the Wailers, Queen, Bruce Springsteen, The Who, and ZZ Top are among the popular recording artists.

DEEP DAFT

A love of horror, rock, musicals, and glam brought Thomas Bangalter and Guy-Manuel de Homem-Christo together—Jimi Hendrix, The Velvet Underground, *Phantom of the Paradise, The Texas Chainsaw Massacre*, KISS, David Bowie, Led Zeppelin, and Pink Floyd, among other favorites.

TECHNO TALK

In 1975, Sony introduced the Betamax video format that, while revolutionary for its time, would become virtually obsolete with the development of the VHS format in Japan by JVC a year later. Although Betamax featured superior quality, Sony could not rival the functionality of VHS machines, and by 1980 JVC's VHS format controlled 70 percent of the North American market.

- David Bowie "Fame," the Eagles's "Best of My Love," and Elton John's cover of The Beatles's "Lucy in the Sky with Diamonds" top the charts.
- NASA launches the Viking 1 planetary probe toward Mars.
- A U.S. Apollo spacecraft docks with a Russian Soyuz spacecraft; astronauts and cosmonauts shake hands in space.
- A young Grandmaster Flash—one of the pioneers of hip-hop—begins DJing

GUY-MANUEL DE HOMEM-CHRISTO

Rumored to be of aristocratic stock, Guy-Manuel de Homem-Christo was born on February 8, 1974, in the Paris suburb of Neuilly-sur-Seine. He is of Portuguese descent—his great-grandfather was the writer Homem Cristo Filho—and his parents were in advertising. He got his first keyboard and a small guitar on Christmas when he was about six or seven years old, but it was when he was fourteen that he received his first "real" instrument: an electric guitar.

DEEP DAFT

Released in 1982, Michael Jackson's groundbreaking album, *Thriller,* was an important influence on the Daft Punk duo—the VHS companion tape also gave Thomas Bangalter and Guy-Manuel de Homem-Christo a glimpse into the creative process—and would be the first album they ever bought with their own money. As de Homem-Christo has said: "It was all Michael Jackson and *Thriller,* all the time."

Paul Williams in *Phantom of the Paradise,* 1974.

FREESTYLE

On June 21, cities around the world celebrate the Fête de la Musique (also known as World Music Day), an annual music festival that traces its roots back to France. In 1981—when Thomas Bangalter and Guy-Manuel de Homem-Christo were only six and seven years old—French composer, music journalist, and radio producer Maurice Fleuret was named director of music and dance of the Ministry of Culture. When Fleuret discovered that a 1982 study on the cultural habits of the French showed that, out of five million people, one child out of two played a musical instrument, he wanted to create a way to share music openly and to encourage amateur and professional musicians to perform on the streets (the only caveat being that all concerts must be free to the public, and all performers must donate their time). A celebration of all kinds of music, from jazz to classical, the first festival took place in Paris in 1982. It would go on to become an international phenomenon, celebrated every June 21 in more than one hundred countries.

The Year Guy-Manuel de Homem-Christo Was Born

▸ Popular films include *The Exorcist, Blazing Saddles, Serpico,* and *Death Wish.* Brian De Palma's *Phantom of the Paradise* opens; this was a film favorite of Thomas Bangalter and Guy-Manuel de Homem-Christo, and one that would introduce them to singer, songwriter, actor, and future collaborator Paul Williams.

▸ Top recording artists are ABBA, The Beach Boys (the compilation album *Endless Summer* surged to the top of the charts), Genesis, The Grateful Dead, Joni Mitchell, The Velvet Underground, Queen, Stevie Wonder, Barry White, and Alice Cooper, among others.

▸ Popular songs: Eric Clapton's cover of Bob Marley's "I Shot the Sheriff," Paul McCartney's "Band on the Run," "You Ain't Seen Nothing Yet" by Bachman-Turner Overdrive, Three Degrees' "When Will I See You Again," and "Kung Fu Fighting" by Carl Douglas.

▸ German electronic band Kraftwerk releases its fourth studio album, *Autobahn.*

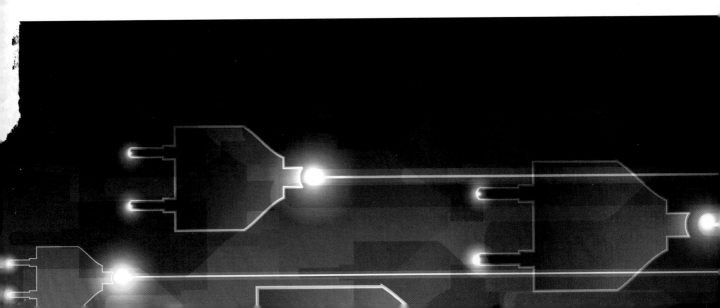

EARLY INFLUENCES

Newcomers to the Daft Punk sound are often surprised to learn that Thomas Bangalter and Guy-Manuel de Homem-Christo's early music influences were more rock and pop than dance. Through the years, the duo's musical tastes have diversified, ranging in artists from Barry Manilow to Kanye West, but in their teen years both men gravitated toward music icons such as The Beach Boys, The Rolling Stones, Pink Floyd, The Velvet Underground, and Led Zeppelin (years later, Daft Punk's mind-blowing live performances would lead one reviewer to describe them as the "Led Zeppelin of dance music").

Thomas Bangalter and Guy-Manuel de Homem-Christo named their first band Darlin' after a song by The Beach Boys: (front, left to right) Mike Love, Brian Wilson, Dennis Wilson, Carl Wilson, and (back) Al Jardine, shown here in 1978.

Initially, however, it was their shared taste in film that made the two fast friends when they met at the Parisian secondary school Lycée Carnot in 1987—the prestigious alma mater of Jacques Chirac, the former president of France. Together, they went to the cinema in the Latin Quarter of Paris on Wednesday and Saturday afternoons; their interests spanned from Charlie Chaplin to Fellini (Bangalter has said the first film they saw together was *The Lost Boys*).

Over time, the artistically inclined chums decided, like many adolescents, to form a band, and they recorded demo tracks with others from their school. In 1992, when Bangalter was seventeen and de Homem-Christo was eighteen, they formed a low-fi French rock band called Darlin' with friend and fellow student Laurent Brancowitz; the band's name was a tribute to a Beach Boys song that was written by Brian Wilson and Mike Love and released on the 1967 album *Wild Honey*. Bangalter played bass guitar, and de Homem-Christo, who provided the vocals, played guitar along with Brancowitz (back then, Bangalter has said, samplers were more expensive than guitars).

Stereolab, shown here in 1996, were a cult favorite 1990s British band known for their cerebral lyrics and experimental sound. They put two songs by Darlin' on a 1993 compilation single.

The trio made a "tape" of a handful of songs that included a cover of The Beach Boys' "Darlin'"—no melody, just the chords—as well as an original composition titled "Cindy So Loud"; both songs were recorded at home with guitars and a drum machine. When the guys heard that Stereolab, an alternative band they liked, was touring in Paris, they managed to pass their tape to the band. Ultimately, Stereolab put both "Darlin'" and "Cindy So Loud" on a compilation single titled *Shimmies in Super 8*, a ragtag of a record featuring songs from groups such as English riot grrrl band Huggy Bear, Colm, and Stereolab itself. The single, released as a double pack with one green and one white vinyl seven-inch, was put out by Stereolab's own United Kingdom label, Duophonic, in 1993—making "Darlin'" and "Cindy So Loud" Bangalter and de Homem-Christo's first commercial releases.

The compilation was largely panned, but there was one bad review, in particular, that would impact Bangalter and de Homem-Christo's career for the next twenty-plus years. Journalist Dave Jennings from *Melody Maker*, a weekly music magazine in the UK, trashed the new record, calling the Darlin' tracks, in particular, "a daft punky thrash."

And that is how the name Daft Punk was born.

Thomas Bangalter and Guy-Manuel de Homem-Christo went helmet-free in their early days.

ORIGINS OF ELECTRONIC DANCE MUSIC

By the time they were in their late teens, Thomas Bangalter and Guy-Manuel de Homem-Christo were growing more interested in electronic dance music, or EDM. With roots in disco and funk (as well as experimental rock and classical music), EDM, in broad terms, is defined as any music that uses electronic instruments or technology to create a seamless flow of sound designed for foot-tapping or booty-shaking entertainment, particularly in nightclub settings.

Kraftwerk in the 1970s.

The synthesizer, a real-time performing musical machine, was an important technological development for the genre because it produces the sounds of a wide variety of instruments, including drums, keyboards, guitars, and horns, and, thus, acted as a stand-in for actual session players. One of the most successful uses of a synthesizer in the early to mid 70s was on a series of collaborative albums by Stevie Wonder and electronic musicians Malcolm Cecil and Robert Margouleff. Cecil and Margouleff designed a large system that was dubbed T.O.N.T.O. (an acronym for The Original New Timbral Orchestra) and which, incidentally, was featured as the "electronic room" in the 1974 film *Phantom of the Paradise.*

Italian producer and composer Giorgio Moroder, a natural behind the console who liked to experiment with new machines and sounds in the early 70s (he was one of the first producers to give digital recording technology a try on his 1979 album *E=MC²*), helped shape the development of electronic music by incorporating synthesizers, specifically the Moog (pronounced MOHG; today,

A Moog displayed at the Musee de la Musique (Music Museum) in Paris, France.

the term Moog is a common generic description for older-generation analog music synthesizers), designed by Dr. Robert Moog, into his compositions. Moroder came across the machine while living in Munich, where classical composer Eberhard Schoener showed him how to use it. Although Moroder has since said that Schoener's use of the Moog was "boring," he was nonetheless so taken with the new sound capability that he wanted to figure out how to incorporate things like synthesizers and sequencers into commercial music for a more exciting sound. Around the same time, two German bands, Kraftwerk and Tangerine Dream, were also experimenting with similar machinery. Kraftwerk's third studio album *Ralf und Florian* (1973) relied more heavily on synthesizers and drum machines than its predecessors, moving Kraftwerk closer to its characteristic sound, and featuring the band's first use of the vocoder, another of its—and, later, Daft Punk's—musical signatures. Likewise, Tangerine Dream's *Phaedra* (1974), the band's fifth studio album, was the first to feature their classic sequencer-driven sound.

THE DAWN OF DISCO

Donna Summer, a trained gospel singer, was an American musical-theater artist living in Munich, Germany, where she performed in a series of stage musicals, including *Hair*. She came to Moroder's attention while doing session work at Musicland, the studio Moroder opened in the basement of his Munich apartment building. At the time, Moroder was working with Pete Bellotte, a British songwriter and record producer (in the late 70s they would go on to form Munich Machine, a collaborative disco project with several studio musicians, including drummer Keith Forsey). Bellotte has said that while doing a sound-check warm-up for a session one day, Forsey employed the then-unique "four-on-the-floor" bass drum pattern, coupled with the "pea soup" (playing an open hi-hat sound and following it with a quick closed sound) rhythm that he had heard on the 1974 dance hit "Rock the Boat" by The Hues Corporation, essentially introducing what were some of the first disco beat elements.

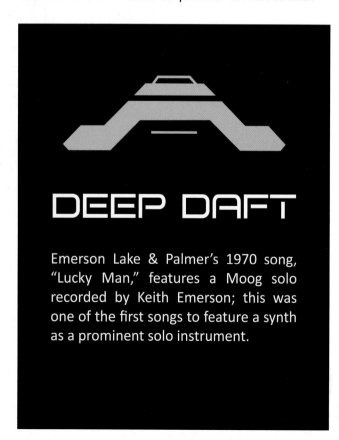

DEEP DAFT

Emerson Lake & Palmer's 1970 song, "Lucky Man," features a Moog solo recorded by Keith Emerson; this was one of the first songs to feature a synth as a prominent solo instrument.

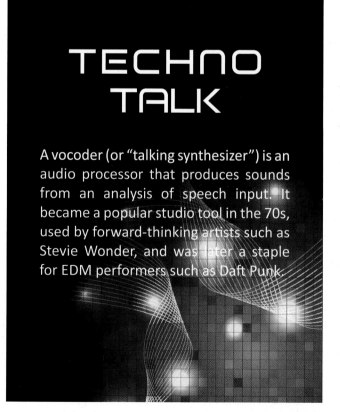

TECHNO TALK

A vocoder (or "talking synthesizer") is an audio processor that produces sounds from an analysis of speech input. It became a popular studio tool in the 70s, used by forward-thinking artists such as Stevie Wonder, and was later a staple for EDM performers such as Daft Punk.

Donna Summer and Giorgio Moroder, creators of the disco hit "Love to Love You Baby."

Kraftwerk, the experimental electronic pop music group formed in Germany, performed with great success in the 1980s.

Networks of members-only parties, clandestine bars, and abandoned warehouse spaces were springing up during this time, ushering in the new dance music. Moroder became interested in developing the new "disco" sound, and he wanted to do some kind of "sexy song" with Summer. She came up with the title "Love to Love You Baby," and together they recorded a demo (Moroder has said that Summer wasn't thrilled with all the groans and heavy breathing, but originally thought she was doing the demo for someone else). When record executives responded favorably to the track—which has come to capture the growingly hedonistic subculture of sex and drugs

TECHNO TALK

In 1970, the Minimoog was invented in response to the growing use of synthesizers in rock and pop music, since large modular synthesizers were pricy, cumbersome, delicate, and not ideal for live performance.

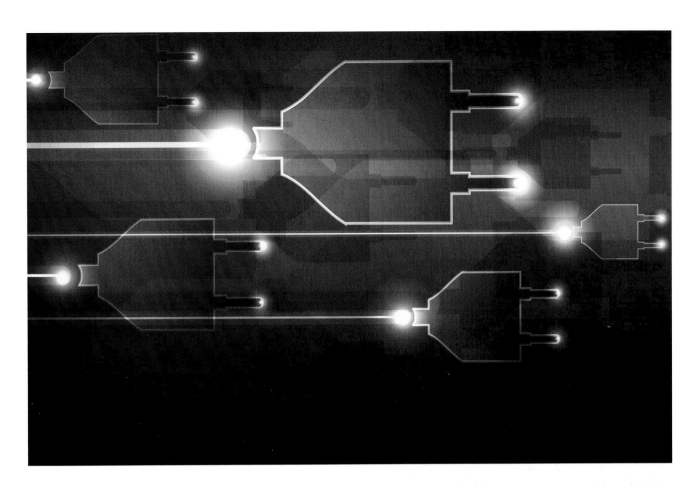

of the period, later epitomized by the renowned Manhattan nightclub, Studio 54—Moroder, Bellotte and Summer rerecorded "Love to Love You Baby," and it was released on an album of the same name in 1975. (Although *Love to Love You Baby* was Summer's second album, it was her first to be released internationally and in the United States. Her first album, *Lady of the Night*, was released only in the Netherlands.) "Love to Love You Baby" went on to become a disco smash on both sides of the Atlantic, although its intense eroticism caused it to be banned by certain radio broadcasters, including the BBC. The song was also one of the first-ever disco hits to be released in an extended form. (In 2013, a new remix of the song was featured on a remix album titled *Love to Love You Donna*.)

Capitalizing on the success of "Love to Love You Baby," Summer returned to America, followed by Moroder (who would eventually base himself on

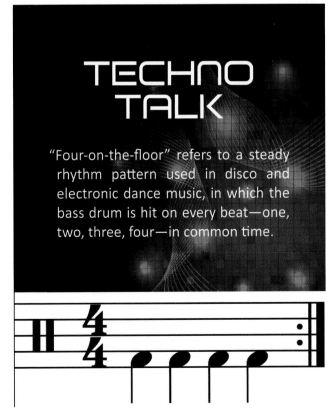

TECHNO TALK

"Four-on-the-floor" refers to a steady rhythm pattern used in disco and electronic dance music, in which the bass drum is hit on every beat—one, two, three, four—in common time.

the West Coast full-time) and Bellotte (who would return to England in the 80s). After recording two more albums in 1976—*Love Trilogy* (which was released a mere eight months after *Love to Love You Baby*) and *Four Seasons of Love*—the following year, the trio released *I Remember Yesterday*, a concept album that would spawn Summer's second Top 10 single, "I Feel Love," a song that was recorded with an entirely synthesized backing track. However, the true magic of "I Feel Love" happened when Moroder asked his studio engineer to create a delay on the bass line—a novel decision that created the song's futuristic and uniquely recognizable rhythm.

The years 1977 and 1978 also saw the release of other synthesizer-heavy tracks, most notably, "Flash Light" by funk band Parliament, with lead vocals by George Clinton, and Kraftwerk's "Trans-Europe Express." What helped dance music really catch on was that rhythm, the hypnotic four-on-the-floor drum beat played to 120 beats per minute (BPM). In fact, the careful calculation of BPM would become vital for DJs who needed to beat-

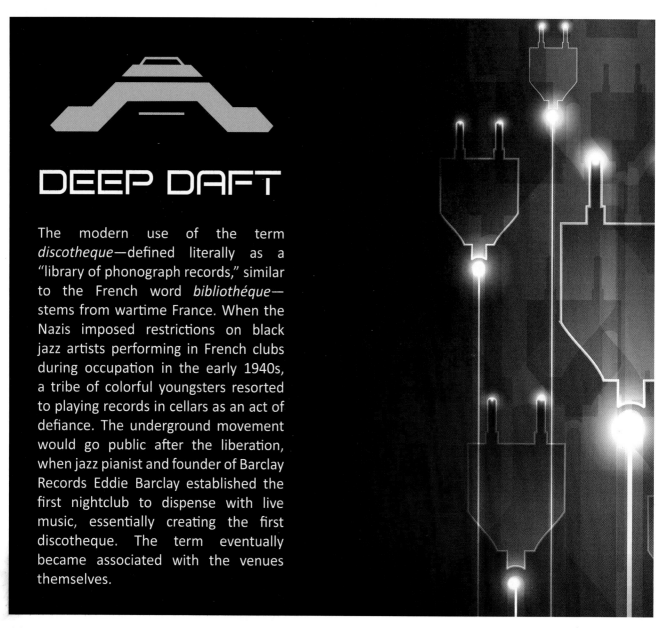

DEEP DAFT

The modern use of the term *discotheque*—defined literally as a "library of phonograph records," similar to the French word *bibliothéque*—stems from wartime France. When the Nazis imposed restrictions on black jazz artists performing in French clubs during occupation in the early 1940s, a tribe of colorful youngsters resorted to playing records in cellars as an act of defiance. The underground movement would go public after the liberation, when jazz pianist and founder of Barclay Records Eddie Barclay established the first nightclub to dispense with live music, essentially creating the first discotheque. The term eventually became associated with the venues themselves.

match and smoothly segue from one song to the next in order to keep the club crowds constantly on their feet.

Although disco began as an underground movement, the genre went mainstream in 1977, the year Steve Rubell and Ian Schrager founded Studio 54 and the wildly popular film *Saturday Night Fever* was released (although some said the film breathed new life into the genre, which was actually on the decline). At this time, disco also started experiencing some crossover appeal—Daft Punk favorites such as Pink Floyd, Queen, KISS, and The Rolling Stones were just a few of the bands to succumb to the genre's immense popularity and influence.

Ultimately, the disco genre started winding down, particularly in the United States, where a strong anti-disco sentiment grew. This culminated on July 12, 1979, which became known as "the day disco died" because of an anti-disco demonstration during a baseball double-header at Comiskey Park in Chicago. At the time of the riot, six of the top

records on the U.S. music charts were disco songs; two months later there were no disco songs to be found on the U.S. Top 10. As disco's popularity declined in the United States, European disco—or "Euro disco," a term first used to describe non-UK disco artists, such as the Swedish group ABBA—continued to evolve throughout the 80s. By the early 90s, the sound had evolved and spun off into a variety of electronic music genres.

DEEP DAFT

Village People, the wild costume-clad disco group that would become an international sensation with the songs "Macho Man" and "Y.M.C.A.," was co-founded by two French composers, Jacques Morali and Henri Belolo.

Donna Summer performing in 1978.

THE BIRTH OF HIP-HOP

While disco was working its way through club culture in the 1970s, another underground urban movement that would come to be known as "hip-hop" was taking shape in New York City. Hip-hop music was both a backlash and successor to disco. As the story goes, Jamaica native DJ Kool Herc (born Clive Campbell), a resident of 1520 Sedgwick Avenue in the South Bronx, would throw parties and bring his sound system to neighboring parks and block parties, offering these events up as an alternative to the violent gang and drug culture of the time. He played hard funk records, isolating the

DJ Kool Herc.

instrumental portions that emphasized the drum beat, the heavily percussive sections known as the "break." Using the same two-turntable setup of DJs who were spinning records in discos, Herc used two copies of the same record to elongate the break. As one record reached the end of the break, he cued the other record back to the beginning, extending that small part of the record into a several-minute loop (essentially, this was an early form of looping). At the time, the word "breaking" was street slang for "getting excited" or "acting energetically." Herc's "breakbeat" DJing would help form the basis of hip-hop music. What's more, Herc's call-outs to his dancers (whom he called "break boys" and "break girls," or, simply, b-boys and b-girls) would lead to the syncopated, rhymed spoken accompaniment that came to be known as rapping.

Herc's DJ style was soon taken up by Grandmaster Flash and Afrika Bambaataa, both of whom are considered pioneers of hip-hop. An electronics student, Flash (born Joseph Saddler) turned DJing into an art form, polishing Herc's style by playing with the electronics of music—instead of using a turntable simply as a playback device, he turned it into a percussion instrument. He was the first DJ to physically lay his hands on a record in order to manipulate its play, marking up the body of the vinyl with grease pencil and crayon, and invented a host of DJing techniques, including Quick Mix Theory, which includes double-back, back-door,

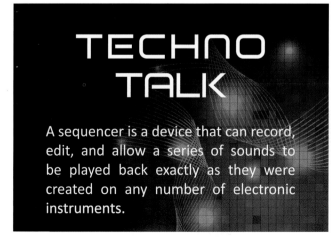

TECHNO TALK

A sequencer is a device that can record, edit, and allow a series of sounds to be played back exactly as they were created on any number of electronic instruments.

DJ Kool Herc, shown here in 2006, is credited with originating hip-hop music.

back-spin, and phasing. Flash's template grew to include cutting, which also spawned scratching (although hip-hop DJ Grand Wizzard Theodore is credited with inventing scratching).

Kevin Donovan (who changed his name to Afrika Bambaataa after winning a trip to Africa, where he was impressed with the Zulu) returned to the Bronx vowing to use hip-hop as a way to draw angry kids out of gangs through a group he founded called the Universal Zulu Nation. Bambaataa is credited with naming the emerging urban culture of music and art of the time as "hip-hop," a phrase that had been used by MCs as part of a scat-inspired style of rhyming. In 1982, Afrika Bambaataa & Soulsonic Force released the seminal track "Planet Rock," a

Afrika Bambaataa, pioneer of hip-hop.

song that blended synthesizer and vocoder sounds with breakbeating. This track is credited with developing the electro style of music, building on the work of early synthpop pioneers Kraftwerk and Yellow Magic Orchestra, a Japanese electronic music band whose cutting-edge production in the late 70s and early 80s made abundant use of synthesizers, samplers, sequencers, drum machines, and digital recording technology as it became available.

In 1979, a New Jersey trio called The Sugarhill Gang released the song "Rapper's Delight," which is considered the first commercially released hip-hop record [although the Fatback Band's "King Tim III (Personality Jock)," a B-side single, was released a few months before and is cited as the beginning of recorded hip-hop]. "Rapper's Delight" was the first hip-hop song to enter the U.S. Top 40. (Blondie's 1981 single "Rapture," which includes a rap performed by lead singer Deborah Harry, became the first single featuring a rap to hit #1.)

"Rapper's Delight" was also the first hip-hop song to make use of sampling, which involves taking a portion (or sample) of a sound recording—in this case Chic's "Good Times"— and reusing it in a different song or piece. Other recording artists were also experimenting with sampling in popular electronic music at this time, including Yellow Magic Orchestra—whose 1978 song "Computer Game/Firecracker" sampled sounds from the video arcade game *Space Invaders*—and Big Audio Dynamite, led by former Clash member Mick Jones, which sampled Clint Eastwood movies on *This Is Big Audio Dynamite* in 1985. That same year, Marley Marl became the first to sample a breakbeat and reprogram it on a song, which would change the way hip-hop beats were made.

"Good Times" was very popular among the DJs of the underground hip-hop culture because its groove was easy to loop while manipulating vinyl on two turntables (today, sampling is done with a "sampler"—an electronic musical instrument

similar to a synthesizer). However, because sampling, as an industry, was brand new, the track was used without authorization. When Chic's Nile Rodgers got wind of it upon hearing an early version of "Rapper's Delight" at a New York City club, he and partner Bernard Edwards threatened legal action over copyright, and were eventually credited as co-writers.

Debbie Harry of Blondie photographed back-stage before a gig at the Spectrum in Philadelphia, on January 21, 1979.

Afrika Bambaataa & Soulsonic Force in 1986.

In the post-disco era, EDM was bolstered once again by technological innovation. In 1982, Musical Instrument Digital Interface (MIDI) became the technical standard for allowing a wide variety of electronic musical instruments and computers—which would become fixtures in multi-track recording studios—to communicate with one another. (The standards resulted from a collaboration between the leading electronic music instrument manufacturers, including Roland and, later, Yamaha, both of which would become innovators in digital technology.) With the development of digital audio, creating and manipulating electronic sounds became simpler, and synthesizers came to dominate the world of pop music in the early 80s. By the end of the decade, dance music made using only electronic instruments became very popular, with the genre splintering into many different subgenres and geographically influenced scenes that continue to evolve to this day, including the following:

Acid House

Originally referring specifically to the mid-80s Chicago house records that used the Roland TB-303 Bass Line synthesizer, acid house is remarkable for its squelching bass sound. The Chicago-based group Phuture's first album *Acid Tracks* (1987) is considered the beginning of the "acid" moniker for the sound, which spread throughout the United Kingdom and continental Europe.

Brostep

An offshoot of the original dubstep (see below) sound, brostep sounds aggressive and harsh, resembling the electric guitar in heavy metal, and replacing dubstep's traditional sub-bass with robotic-sounding and fluctuating midrange frequencies.

Drum & Bass

With an emphasis on drum work and bass line, this genre offers fast breakbeats (160 to 180 BPMs). Like dubstep, it began as an offshoot of the hardcore early-90s UK rave scene, and is characterized by its edgy percussion, speed, and heavy bass lines. (The jungle genre of EDM falls into this category, as well.)

Dub

Synonymous with its name, dub music, which grew out of reggae music in the 60s, plays with versions of existing songs (similar to a remix). The genre often drops lead vocals and instruments, emphasizing the stripped-down drum and bass parts, and employing sound work, such as echoes.

Dubstep

This subgenre started as an underground reaction to the commercialization of UK garage music in the late 90s, which had lost its darker instrumental sound. Producers such as El-B, Horsepower Productions, and Oris Jay created experimental remixes, or dubs, of two-step garage releases, spawning a new subgenre that was bass heavy. Notably, producers such as Skrillex, who have taken dubstep mainstream, feature more of a wobble bass (an extended, musically manipulated bass note) and turbocharged sound.

Electro

With influences ranging from Kraftwerk (considered the forefathers of pure electro), Yellow Magic Orchestra, Gary Numan, Afrika Bambaataa, and Herbie Hancock, among others, electro (or electro-funk) blends lots of drum machines, sampling, video-game and robotic sounds, and, in later years,

Korg micro synthesizer.

full-bodied synths. Most electro is instrumental or utilizes vocals processed through a vocoder.

Freestyle

With origins in the United States in the mid 80s, freestyle (aka "breakdancing" music) is a form of hip-hop dance that, like electro, originated from the electro-funk of Afrika Bambaataa & Soulsonic Force's 1982 seminal track "Planet Rock," as well as other radio-friendly songs, such as Shannon's "Let the Music Play." The style is characterized by Latin percussion and heavy syncopation, as well as themes of romance, love, and having a good time.

Garage

Named in reference to the New York City club the Paradise Garage, this subgenre of house music emphasizes quick vocal samples. Although American producer Todd Edwards is considered the originator of the sound, once it was brought to the UK and played at a slightly faster tempo, the genre exploded.

House

American-born and one of the most popular forms of EDM, house music grew in Chicago in the early-80s aftermath of disco; it is influenced by disco's percussive, repetitive four-on-the-floor beat. New York DJ Frankie Knuckles—considered the godfather of house music—started enhancing disco tracks with drum machine beats and tape edits at Chicago's Warehouse Nightclub, where he was invited to play in the early 80s, and house music was born. In 1983, Jesse Saunders released *On and On*, generally regarded as the first Chicago house record.

DEEP DAFT

Modern remixing—whereby a song is edited to sound different from its original version (in pitch or tempo, for example)—found its roots in the Jamaican dance hall culture of the late 60s and early 70s. Soon DJs in early discos were using similar tricks to keep the music going and people on the dance floor. In the late 60s, unhappy with the DJ's performance at a bar/restaurant called The Sandpiper on Fire Island, New York, Tom Moulton (a model with a few music industry jobs under his belt) put together his own mix, a reel-to-reel tape of overlapping songs, which gained the attention of the New York music industry. His work in the industry would earn him a reputation as the father of the disco mix. He also was the innovator of the twelve-inch single vinyl format and the breakdown or "disco break"— the part of the song where instruments have a solo, providing a rhythm-only section that allowed DJs to begin mixing in the next record to be played.

DEEP DAFT

In the late 80s and early 90s, warehouse parties, raves, and outdoor festival scenes became offshoots of the 70s nightclub scene, showcasing the latest trends in EDM.

Moombahton

One recent subgenre of EDM, Moombahton, emerged in 2009 and was created by Dave Nada, a Washington, D.C.-based DJ. As the story goes, Nada was DJing a party when he took a track he liked, Afrojack's remix of "Moombah," and slowed it down from 128 BPM to around 108 BPM, which created the basis for the genre.

Rave

Rave found its origins in England's acid house movement, when authorities were clamping down on London clubs, prompting the parties—or raves, as they became known—to move out to the countryside. As the parties grew bigger and as Europeans began to produce their own house records, "rave" came to symbolize the music as well as the venues.

Techno

Inspired by Kraftwerk and New York electro, techno stems from a small network of kids in Detroit—in particular, Juan Atkins, who is credited as the originator of techno music. Atkins and partner Rick Davis formed Cybotron, a group inspired by Midwestern funk, notably George Clinton, as well as Kraftwerk, Yellow Magic Orchestra, and others, fusing austere European techno-pop with street-level funk. In 1985, Atkins formed Metroplex Records and released "No UFOs," which created a blueprint for techno. Goldie's 1992 track, "Terminator," pioneered the technique of time-stretching, the process of changing the speed or duration of an audio signal without affecting its pitch, for hardcore techno.

Trance

Originating in Germany in the 90s, trance is a variant of techno and is known for its anthems—huge tracks with relentlessly hypnotic riffs that build up and down.

70s
Disco, Europe
Dub, Jamaica
Hip-Hop, U.S. (New York)

80s
Acid House, U.S. (Chicago)
Electro, U.S. (New York)
Freestyle, U.S.
Garage, UK
House, U.S. (Chicago)
Techno, U.S. (Detroit)

90s
Dubstep, UK
Drum & Bass, UK
Rave
Trance, Germany

00s
Moombahton, U.S.

10s
Brostep, U.S.

FORMING THE DUO

As the UK rave scene filtered across the English Channel in the late 80s and early 90s, Thomas Bangalter and Guy-Manuel de Homem-Christo developed more of an interest in electronic dance music. They were drawn to bands such as Stone Roses and Happy Mondays, pioneering groups of the Manchester, England, music scene (known as "Madchester"), which mixed alternative rock, psychedelic rock, and dance music. (The Second Summer of Love is the name given to the late 80s period in Britain characterized by an explosion of acid house music and drug-fueled rave parties.) In particular, two releases got Bangalter and de Homem-Christo's attention: Primal Scream's ground-breaking album *Screamadelica* (1991), which mixed rock and roll classicism with the looser elements of dance, and "Soon," the closing track to My Bloody Valentine's 1991 album, *Loveless*, which featured a dance-oriented beat behind guitarist Kevin Shields's glide-guitar playing after the band signed with Virgin Records, which was owned at the time by Thorn EMI.

Bangalter and de Homem-Christo purchased electronic recording equipment using money Bangalter received for his eighteenth birthday and began experimenting with making house music based on big hip-hop beats in Bangalter's bedroom. Soon, Darlin', the rock-oriented band they had formed with Laurent Brancowitz, disbanded, and Brancowitz went on to join his brother Christian Mazzalai's alternative rock group, which came to be known as Phoenix. (Bangalter, de Homem-Christo, and Brancowitz remained friends—Daft

Punk made a surprise appearance during the encore of a Phoenix concert at Madison Square Garden in October 2010.)

In 1993, Bangalter and de Homem-Christo were at a rave party at EuroDisney, where they met the managers of the Scottish EDM label, Soma Records, which was cofounded a couple of years prior by the electronic music duo Slam, composed of Stuart Macmillan and Orde Meikle. Bangalter presented a demo of his and de Homem-Christo's work to Macmillan under the Daft Punk moniker, and in 1994, Daft Punk released its first single, "The New Wave" (part of a four-track EP), on Soma—the song was released again later that year on the UMM label under license from Soma and would eventually evolve into "Alive," a track that appeared on Daft Punk's debut studio album *Homework*.

"Da Funk," an instrumental disco track by Daft Punk, became the duo's first commercially successful song. Initially released by the Soma label as a single in 1995 (with the B-side "Rollin' & Scratchin'," which would reappear on Daft Punk's first album, *Homework*), "Da Funk" was released again (with the B-side "Musique," which would reappear on the compilation album *Musique Vol. 1 1993–2005*) in late 1996 after the band signed with Virgin Records.

Bangalter has said that "Da Funk" was made after listening to West Coast G-funk, or gangsta-funk, a subgenre of hip-hop, for weeks (although he has noted that while comparisons have been made to Queen, The Clash, and Giorgio Moroder, no one seemed to agree with Bangalter and de Homem-Christo that the track sounded like hip-hop). With its filtered disco beat and 70s sound effects, "Da Funk" was named by *Pitchfork*, the Chicago-based Internet publication devoted to music criticism and commentary, as one of the Top 200 tracks of the 90s and—with help from a memorable video directed by Spike Jonze and starring Charles, an anthropomorphic dog—would become one of the most popular tracks on *Homework*.

DEEP DAFT

French house, a catchall term for house music produced by French artists, became popular in the late 90s. Driven by a steady four-on-the-floor rhythm, the sound is defined by a heavy reliance on filtering and phasing (whereby a repetitive phrase is played on two musical instruments, in steady but not identical tempo, to create an echo, doubling, and ringing effect) on samples from late 70s and early 80s American or European disco tracks. Recording artists Daft Punk, Cassius (consisting of producing team Philippe Zdar and Boom Bass), and Stardust (a collaborative trio featuring Bangalter), became three of the first internationally successful artists of the genre.

France's Ed Banger Records, said to be one of the most influential labels in electronic music, was founded in 2003 by Pedro Winter (also known as Busy P) who, in addition to being a DJ, producer, and recording artist, served as manager for Daft Punk from 1996 to 2008. Winter met Thomas Bangalter and Guy-Manuel de Homem-Christo when he was a law student in 1996, and the duo asked him to work with them. In 2002, Winter, whose musical influences ranged from heavy metal to rock and hip-hop, created Headbangers Entertainment, through which he also managed French electronic artists, such as Cassius and DJ Mehdi.

A year later, Winter founded Ed Banger, a label that touts artists such as Breakbot, Feadz, and French dance duo Justice, which signed with the label after creating a remix of the song "Never Be Alone" by now defunct British electro-rock group Simian for a 2003 contest hosted by a Paris college radio station. The track became a hit in clubs and on the Internet, prompting Ed Banger's sharp rise to fame in early 2007. (The video of the track, re-titled "We Are Your Friends" by Justice vs. Simian, won Best Video at the 2006 MTV Europe Music Awards; Kanye West crashed the stage during the video director's acceptance speech after his video for the song "Touch the Sky" failed to win.)

The following year, Winter stopped managing Daft Punk to focus more on his label and music career. In addition to running the label, he continues to make music, and, as Busy P, has released five singles, most recently "Still Busy," which dropped in June 2013.

Pedro Winter, aka Busy P.

HOMEWORK

Homework, Daft Punk's first studio album, released in January 1997, was recorded in Thomas Bangalter's bedroom (he had to move the bed to another room in order to make space for all the gear). In addition to creating innovative music, with this album Bangalter and Guy-Manuel de Homem-Christo set out to show that music can be a do-it-yourself proposition, made in the same way that two young kids might work together on a school assignment. Indeed, the album's artwork, designed by de Homem-Christo, is youth-oriented, displaying the now-familiar Daft Punk logo as a patch sewn onto a black satin jacket on the cover and an inner-sleeve photograph—made to look as if it is inside the unzipped satin jacket—showcasing a desk cluttered with various adolescent objects that double as Daft Punk reference points, including a 1976 KISS poster and a Chic single sleeve.

Homework's gatefold sleeve features a photo spread of an adolescent's desk filled with all kinds of hints and references relating to Daft Punk.

1. A radio: For the track "WDPK 83.7 FM"
2. Cassette labeled "Funk Number 1": For the track "Da Funk" (and, of course, "Funk Ad")
3. Gold ornament of a phoenix: For the track "Phoenix" as well as the musical group featuring friend and former bandmate Laurent Brancowitz
4. Beach Boys album: For the iconic California band, The Beach Boys, a major influence on Daft Punk
5. The word "Darlin'": For both the Beach Boys song and Thomas Bangalter and Guy-Manuel de Homem-Christo's first band together
6. Globe: For the track "Around The World"
7. 45 on a turntable: For the track "Rollin' & Scratchin'"
8. Notebook labeled "Homework": For the album itself and, perhaps, the track "Teachers"
9. Magazine page featuring the headline, "Up Your Fidelity": For the song "High Fidelity"

10. *Playboy*: For the track "Oh Yeah" (The way the magazine is positioned, with the center seam running through the B, the magazine name reads PLAY OY, with the O and Y representing the words "Oh Yeah.")

11. Box of matches: For the track "Burnin'"

12. Silver coins: For the track "Indo Silver Club"

13. KISS poster: For KISS, a musical influence, and "Alive," a *Homework* track

14. Stickers of Led Zeppelin and The Who: For the English rock bands, both musical influences

15. Chic's 1982 "Stage Fright"/"So Fine": For Chic, a longtime musical influence

16. Electrical jack: Representing Daft Punk's fascination with technology

17. Childhood photos of Thomas Bangalter and Guy-Manuel de Homem-Christo

18. Andy Gibb pencil holder: For the youngest Gibb brother (sibling to Barry, Robin, and Maurice) of whom Daft Punk was a fan.

19. Dr Pepper can: For the initials "D" and "P," which stand for "Daft Punk"

At heart, *Homework* is an ode to electronic dance music filtered through Daft Punk's love of classic rock—the duo has said the album is their way of telling their Darlin' rock fans, "Hey, electronic music is cool." Upon its release, Homework got lots of buzz on the club scene, as well as major promotional support from Virgin Records, Daft Punk's label. Because the duo originally wanted the majority of its pressings to be in vinyl, only 50,000 albums were printed in CD format, but overwhelming sales caused production to accelerate. *Homework*, featuring sixteen tracks, became so popular that it was distributed in thirty-five countries, placed on the Billboard 200 and the UK Top 10 album charts, and brought worldwide attention to French house music, helping to make Daft Punk one of the biggest-selling acts to come out of France. Here are some of the album's biggest tracks.

With a name that has furrowed a few brows, "Daftendirekt," the album's first track, is thought to mean "Daft live" (Daft en direct), referring to the fact that it is a live track, recorded at a fuse party in Ghent, Belgium, according to the album's liner notes. Noted for its vocoder voices that beckon, "Dafunk back to the punk, c'mon," which is repeated throughout the song, "Daftendirekt"—

TRACKLIST

"Daftendirekt"

"WDPK 83.7 FM"

"Revolution 909"

"Da Funk"

"Phoenix"

"Fresh"

"Around the World"

"Rollin' & Scratchin'"

"Teachers"

"High Fidelity"

"Rock 'n Roll"

"Oh Yeah"

"Burnin'"

"Indo Silver Club"

"Alive"

"Funk Ad"

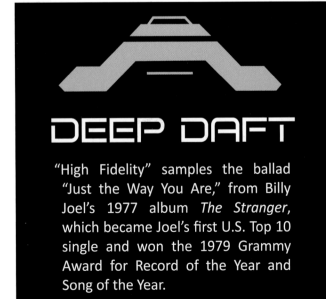

DEEP DAFT

"High Fidelity" samples the ballad "Just the Way You Are," from Billy Joel's 1977 album *The Stranger*, which became Joel's first U.S. Top 10 single and won the 1979 Grammy Award for Record of the Year and Song of the Year.

ROBO OP

The liner notes of *Homework* include a mask-less shot of Daft Punk, who were still showing their faces in public in 1997. It was sometime between the release of *Homework* and the duo's next studio album, *Discovery*, that Thomas Bangalter and Guy-Manuel de Homem-Christo started to keep their identities hidden with various face-obscuring masks when attending media-related events.

DEEP DAFT

Roman Coppola, director of Daft Punk's "tomato video," stems from the renowned Coppola family—his father, Francis Ford Coppola, and sister, Sofia Coppola, are Academy Award winners, and his cousin Nicolas Cage was nominated for Best Actor for 1995's *Leaving Las Vegas*. He directed many music videos for The Strokes, whose frontman Julian Casablancas collaborated with Daft Punk on *Random Access Memories*.

Roman Coppola, shown here at the 2013 Writers Guild Awards in Los Angeles.

which samples the Vaughan Mason & Crew 1979 song "Bounce, Rock, Skate, Roll" (which, in turn, samples Chic's "Good Times")—provided the name for Daft Punk's promotional tour for *Homework*, Daftendirektour 1997, in which most of the songs from the album were mixed together.

At only twenty-eight seconds (practically the length of a ringtone), "WDPK 83.7 FM" is the shortest track on *Homework*. The song features elements from the song "Da Funk" and lyrics from "Musique," an earlier release of Daft Punk's. The title is thought to be a wordplay—the D and P referring to the band's name and replacing the O and R in "work." The track repeats the French term, *musique*, nine times before fading into a backing track under a DJ-type voiceover (reportedly Bangalter's) that begins: "WDPK 83.7, the sound of tomorrow." The track then fades out as "Revolution 909" begins.

"Revolution 909," a thumping instrumental track, is a nod to the Roland TR-909, a rhythm composing machine that proved vital to the growth of electronic music. However, the track's title may also have some political connotations: Bangalter has said that the French government, which had a tendency to clamp down on rave parties, didn't understand the genre of electronic dance music like they did rock music. Daft Punk explored this theme in the "Revolution 909" music video, directed by Roman Coppola. The video opens with a rave party in an alley, and when the police arrive to break it up, an officer confronts a woman who looks as if she will be arrested. The woman notices a tomato sauce stain on the police officer's shirt, which triggers a flashback of the entire lifecycle of that tomato sauce: The tomato seed is planted, sprouts, is harvested, packaged with other tomatoes, brought to a grocery store, bought by a woman, prepared into sauce (with cooking show–like subtitles enumerating the recipe steps), poured over pasta, placed in a Tupperware container, and then into a brown paper bag. The bag is shown with the officer in his squad car and, while eating, he unknowingly gets some sauce on his shirt. The flashback ends and the officer, seeing the young woman staring at his shirt, looks down at the stain, which gives the woman the opportunity to escape when someone pulls her up onto a second-story platform.

"Da Funk"—the instrumental track that was first released as a single on the Soma label—and its accompanying video are considered to be classic 90s house music. (The song, like "Daftendirekt," samples Vaughan Mason & Crew's 1979 song "Bounce, Rock, Skate, Roll" and "I'm Gonna Love You Just a Little More Baby" by Barry White.)

Prior to its inclusion on *Homework*, "Indo Silver Club" was released as a single in 1996 on the duo's previous label, Soma Records. Because the track had no artist credit, it was thought to have been created by the nonexistent producers Indo Silver

Club. "Indo Silver Club" features a sample of the 1978 chart-topping disco single "Hot Shot," by Karen Young.

Directed by Spike Jonze, the "Da Funk" music video, entitled *"Big City Nights,"* focuses on the character of Charles, who would become nearly synonymous with the Daft Punk brand. Charles is an anthropomorphic dog played by Tony Maxwell. The drummer for the band That Dog from 1991 to 1997, Maxwell is a frequent collaborator of Jonze's (he choreographed the Dance of Despair and Disillusionment in Jonze's *Being John Malkovich*), and has worked as a film composer.

As the video begins, Charles is walking along a bustling New York City street on a crutch (his leg is in a cast) and carrying a boom box blasting "Da Funk" (the volume knob, apparently, is broken). Throughout the video, Charles appears down on

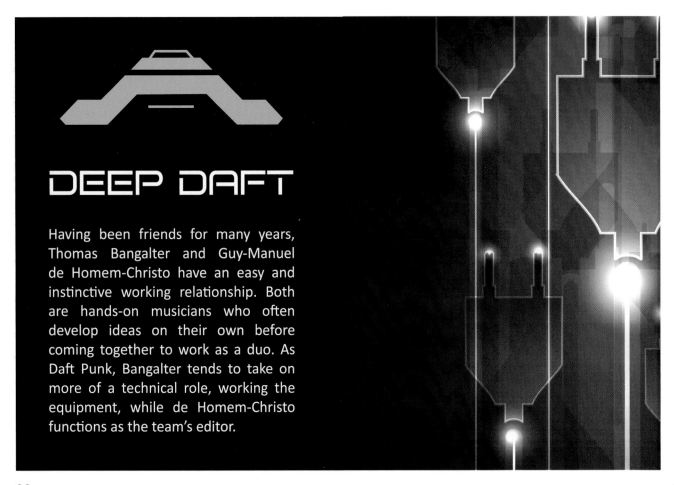

DEEP DAFT

Having been friends for many years, Thomas Bangalter and Guy-Manuel de Homem-Christo have an easy and instinctive working relationship. Both are hands-on musicians who often develop ideas on their own before coming together to work as a duo. As Daft Punk, Bangalter tends to take on more of a technical role, working the equipment, while de Homem-Christo functions as the team's editor.

his luck—he is made fun of by two boys, is turned down when he tries to participate in a public survey (he hasn't lived in the neighborhood long enough), and his music annoys a street bookseller . . . although the good-natured Charles buys a paperback novel, also titled *Big City Nights*, anyway. Things are looking up for Charles when he reconnects with Beatrice, a childhood neighbor, at a grocery store. He and Beatrice decide to have dinner together at her home, but at the end of the video Charles is left standing at a bus stop; he is unable to board with his volume-challenged boom box because of a sign that says "no radios."

The track "Fresh" is intended to be breezy and light with a comical structure (it opens with the sound of lapping waves). The accompanying video, directed by Daft Punk itself, marks the return of Charles the dog-faced man from Daft Punk's "Da Funk" video. (As with "Da Funk," "Fresh" serves as a score against which the story of the video plays out.) This time around, Charles is an actor who is shooting scenes for a film that is set on a beach (Daft Punk has said they wanted Charles to be shown in happier times in order to cheer up fans who saw him as dejected and sad in "Da Funk"). When the day's shoot is over, Charles discusses techniques with his director (a cameo by Spike Jonze) and runs into Beatrice, whom he has apparently been seeing since she left him at the bus stop at the end of "Da Funk." The two kiss, make plans to go to a restaurant for dinner, and drive off into the sunset in Beatrice's red convertible.

The key hook of "Around the World" is a steady synth bass line (inspired by Chic's "Good Times") and a robotic voice repeatedly singing "around the world" (the phrase occurs 144 times throughout the album version of the song). The video, directed by Michel Gondry, is a visual interpretation of music played on a vinyl record: Four robots walk in a circle on a platform, four tall athletes wearing

George Clinton.

DEEP DAFT

Daft Punk pays homage to many of its inspirations on *Homework:* The track "Teachers" name-checks more than forty musical influences, including Brian Wilson, George Clinton, Lil Louis, DJ Sneak, Romanthony, Dr. Dre, and Todd Edwards. Also, DJ Deelat and DJ Crabbe appear on the track "Oh Yeah."

track suits with small prosthetic heads go up and down stairs, four women dressed like synchronized swimmers (or, as Gondry calls them, "disco girls") move up and down another set of stairs, four skeletons dance in the center of the "record," and four mummies dance in time to the song's drum pattern. Each group of four is meant to represent a different instrument—singing (the robots), bass guitar (athletes), keyboard (disco girls), guitar (skeletons), and drums (mummies).

"Burnin'," a relentlessly looped instrumental track, samples the bass line of "Down to Love Town," by Motown group The Originals, and is embellished with an array of electronic swoops and swirls. The video, directed by French photographer and director Seb Janiak, was shot in a Chicago office building at One South Wacker Drive, and features a party scene that pays homage to the Chicago house producers who inspired Daft Punk—DJ Sneak, Roger Sanchez, Junior Sanchez, Derrick Carter, Roy Davis Jr., Paul Johnson, Robert Armani, and DJ Hyperactive, all of whom make appearances. Bangalter and de Homem-Christo make brief cameos as well—Bangalter is wearing sunglasses and a long-haired, dark wig, while de Homem-Christo sports sunglasses, a red suit, and a blond wig.

DEEP DAFT

Perhaps best known for his collaborations with screenwriter Charlie Kaufman (*Being John Malkovich* and *Adaptation*), Spike Jonze is an American director, producer, screenwriter, and actor (he has a cameo as Charles's director in the Daft Punk–directed video for "Fresh"). He is the co-creator and executive producer of MTV's *Jackass*, and has directed music videos for many recording artists, including Weezer, the Beastie Boys, Björk, and Fatboy Slim, among others. He also created the *Directors Label* series, devoted to notable music video directors, with filmmakers Chris Cunningham and Michel Gondry, a fellow *Homework* collaborator.

Director Spike Jonze.

Michel Gondry, who directed Daft Punk's "Around the World" music video, at the Deauville American Film Festival.

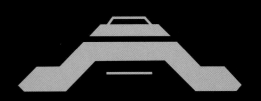

DEEP DAFT

Michel Gondry is an Academy Award–winning French filmmaker (he won Best Screenplay for *Eternal Sunshine of the Spotless Mind*, for which Charlie Kaufman served as screenwriter), as well as a commercial and music video director and screenwriter. Known for his inventive visual style and for making full use of *mise en scène*, as he does in Daft Punk's "Around the World" video, he has directed music videos for Björk, The White Stripes, The Chemical Brothers, The Vines, Radiohead, and Beck, among others.

DEEP DAFT

Homework's final track, "Funk Ad," is essentially (as the song title implies) "Da Funk" played backwards.

D.A.F.T.: A STORY ABOUT DOGS, ANDROIDS, FIREMEN AND TOMATOES

ANCHORED BY the easily recognizable—and much beloved—image of Charles the anthropomorphic dog, the album cover of *D.A.F.T.: A Story About Dogs, Androids, Firemen and Tomatoes* is a visual representation of the colorful, fun, wide-ranging, and somewhat off-the-wall assortment of music that would come to symbolize the Daft Punk brand.

D.A.F.T.: A Story About Dogs, Androids, Firemen and Tomatoes, released in 1999, is a video collection for Daft Punk's debut album, *Homework,* and features music videos for six tracks: "Da Funk," "Fresh," "Around the World," "Burnin'," "Revolution 909," and "Rollin' & Scratchin'." There is no cohesive plot that connects any of the videos, although the title references elements or themes found within five of them—dogs ("Da Funk" and "Fresh"), androids ("Around the Word"), firemen ("Burnin'"), and tomatoes ("Revolution 909"). The only exception is "Rollin' & Scratchin'," the video for which consists of a live performance of the song in Los Angeles. (The video was also released on the special bonus DVD edition of the *Musique Vol. 1 1993–2005* compilation album. The DVD edition features a multiple camera angle video, which allows viewers to select camera shots to create their own unique edit.)

The video collection's bonus material is plentiful and embodies the same playful spirit found in Daft Punk's music. It includes behind-the-scenes footage, commentaries, production material, and unreleased remixes. For "Da Funk," there's audio commentary with director Spike Jonze, plus a making-of video set to an Armand Van Helden remix and another, featuring the song "On da Rocks" by Thomas Bangalter (released on his Roulé label) that offers a behind-the-scenes look at the making of the Charles dog head. Michel Gondry, who directed "Around the World," provides audio commentary and gives classroom pointers—with a chalkboard and all—on the theories behind that song's video; a complementary video features a Masters at Work remix.

The videos for "Burnin'," directed by Seb Janiak, and "Revolution 909," directed by Roman Coppola, feature an Ian Pooly mix and a Roger Sanchez remix (both directors provide audio commentary), while the video for "Fresh," directed by Daft Punk, showcases rehearsal footage as well as behind-the-scenes fun.

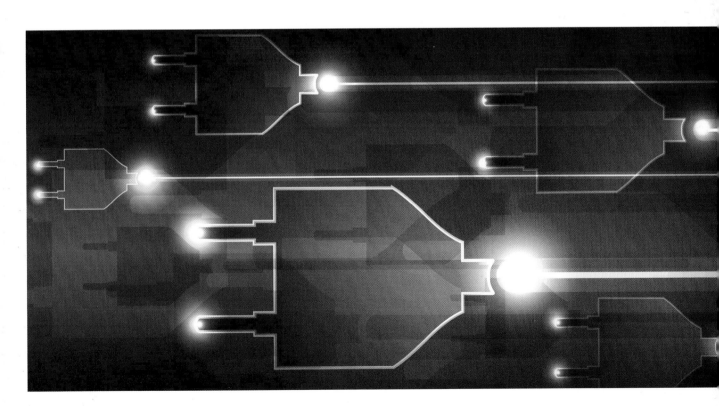

ALIVE 1997

In 1997, Daft Punk embarked on a tour in support of their debut studio album *Homework*. Initially called "Daftendirektour 1997," the tour was later renamed "Alive 1997" and took the pair to the UK, France, Sweden, Belgium, Norway, the United States, Germany, the Netherlands, and Denmark.

DAFT PUNK performed two Alive tours over the course of their career, each receiving its own dedicated live album. While the cover of *Alive 1997* resembled a trunk and featured a stenciled album title (one can imagine the words "Fragile: Handle with Care" in its place), the image chosen for *Alive 2007*, shown here, references the central pyramid of the duo's groundbreaking tour of the same year amid a very *Tron*-like grid of dissecting lines.

A forty-five-minute excerpt of the tour—performed at the Que Club in Birmingham, England, on November 8, 1997 (and said to be Daft Punk's favorite performance of the tour)—was made into a live album that was initially released as part of Daft Club, an online music service free for those who bought early versions of the duo's second studio album *Discovery*. Early pressings of *Discovery* contained a Daft Club membership card that granted access to the Daft Club Web site, which contained remixes and the live recording. (The Daft Club service ended in January 2003.)

The album was later titled *Alive 1997* and released in October 2001 on Virgin Records (the CD and vinyl packaging included a set of Daft Punk stickers). Without a tracklisting and running as one continuous track, *Alive 1997* features a marathon mixing of Daft Punk songs that includes elements of "Daftendirekt," "Da Funk," "Rollin' & Scratchin'," and "Alive" from the *Homework* album, all performed with unique improvisation and fluid tempo shifts. Also featured are elements of Armand Van Helden's "Ten Minutes of Funk" remix of "Da Funk" as well as what would become the track "Short Circuit" on the *Discovery* album. *Alive 1997* peaked at number twenty-five on the French albums chart in 2001.

DEEP DAFT

As a general music rule, live albums tend not to be regarded as highly or to sell as well as studio albums (in *Rolling Stone*'s 2003 list of the 500 Greatest Albums of All Time, only eighteen were live albums). However, in some select circumstances live albums have rivaled—and even exceeded—sales of studio albums, as was the case with *Alive!* by KISS, one of Daft Punk's musical influences, and Peter Frampton's *Frampton Comes Alive!*. To date, country music superstar Garth Brooks, whose *Double Live* album sold in excess of 21 million copies, holds the record for the best-selling live album worldwide.

Armand Van Helden (left) with A Trak.

DEEP DAFT

Armand Van Helden, a New York City–based DJ and producer, has remixed a variety of Platinum artists, including The Rolling Stones, Katy Perry, P. Diddy, Janet Jackson, Britney Spears, and Tori Amos.

GOING SOLO

In the mid to late 90s, around the time Daft Punk released their debut album *Homework* and began touring, Thomas Bangalter and Guy-Manuel de Homem-Christo embarked on solo endeavors, passion projects that provided a vehicle for music that they felt didn't quite fit into the Daft Punk style.

THOMAS BANGALTER

In 1995, Thomas Bangalter founded the label Roulé ("rolled," in French), which he has referred to as more of an "outlet" than an official label. Roulé's roster of musicians includes Romanthony (who would also collaborate with Daft Punk on their second album, *Discovery*), Stardust, Roy Davis Jr., DJ Falcon (a longtime friend and future *Random Access Memories* collaborator), Alan Braxe, and Together, a band consisting of Falcon and Bangalter that released the single "So Much Love to Give" in 2003. Bangalter also produced solo music on Roulé: two EPs, *Trax on da Rocks*, and *Trax on da Rocks Vol. 2,* released in 1995 and

1998. (The track "On da Rocks" was featured in a behind-the-scenes video for "Da Funk" that was included with *D.A.F.T.: A Story About Dogs, Androids, Firemen and Tomatoes,* and the songs "Outrun," "Extra Dry," and "Turbo" later appeared in the video game *Midnight Club II.*)

Roulé's single, "Music Sounds Better With You" by Stardust, was arguably the label's biggest hit, reaching #1 on the dance charts in many European countries. Stardust consisted of Benjamin Diamond (vocals), Alan Braxe (music), and Bangalter (production).

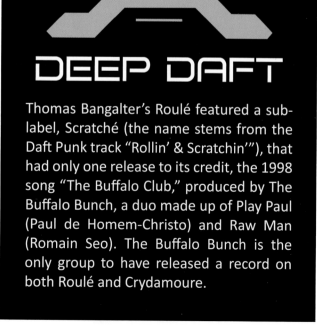

DEEP DAFT

Thomas Bangalter's Roulé featured a sub-label, Scratché (the name stems from the Daft Punk track "Rollin' & Scratchin'"), that had only one release to its credit, the 1998 song "The Buffalo Club," produced by The Buffalo Bunch, a duo made up of Play Paul (Paul de Homem-Christo) and Raw Man (Romain Seo). The Buffalo Bunch is the only group to have released a record on both Roulé and Crydamoure.

ROULÉ DISCOGRAPHY

Release Date	Title	Artist
1995	*Trax on da Rocks* (featuring the tracks "On Da Rocks," "Roulé Boulé," "What to Do," "Outrun," and "Ventura")	Thomas Bangalter
1996	"Spinal Scratch"	Thomas Bangalter
1997	"Vertigo"	Alan Braxe
1998	"Rock Shock"	Roy Davis Jr.
1998	"Music Sounds Better With You"	Stardust
1998	*Trax on da Rocks Vol. 2* (featuring the tracks "Club Soda," "Extra Dry," "Shuffle!," "Colossus," and "Turbo")	Thomas Bangalter
1999	"Hold On"	Romanthony
1999	*Hello, My Name Is DJ Falcon* (featuring the tracks "First," "Honeymoon," "Untitled," and "Unplugged")	DJ Falcon
2000	"Together"	Together
2002	"So Much Love to Give"	Together
2002	*Irréversible* (soundtrack for the film *Irréversible*)	Thomas Bangalter
2003	"Outrage"	Thomas Bangalter

Additionally, Bangalter, who had a burgeoning interest in filmmaking, produced the score for the film *Irréversible* (a 2002 French thriller written and directed by Gaspar Noé) under the Roulé label. A soundtrack album of the same name was later released. It featured three of Bangalter's *Trax on da Rocks* songs—"Outrun," "Ventura," and "Extra Dry"—in addition to works by Gustav Mahler, Étienne Daho, and Beethoven (however, North American pressings of the album featured only the Bangalter tracks).

Outside of Roulé, Bangalter was featured with French hip-hop group 113 on the track "113 Fout La Merde" in 2002. He also served as the sound effects director for the 2009 film *Enter the Void*, his second collaboration with Noé. (Bangalter was initially approached by Noé to compose the film's entire soundtrack, but had to decline because he was working with de Homem-Christo on the *TRON: Legacy* score.)

Additionally, in 2011, Bangalter directed and choreographed a short film featuring Élodie Bouchez (a French actress and Bangalter's wife), which served as an advertisement for the fashion line Co. The following year, he scored the short film *First Point*, directed by Richard Phillips and starring Lindsay Lohan.

GUY-MANUEL
DE HOMEM-CHRISTO

In 1997, Guy-Manuel de Homem-Christo co-founded the Crydamoure label—which was named after a variation of the French phrase *cri d'amour* (or "shout of love," in English)—with Pumpking Records' Eric Chedeville (also known as DJ Rico), with whom he also makes music under the group name Le Knight Club. Crydamoure, which has been called a "more coherently disco influenced" label than Roulé, released singles by Le Knight Club; Paul Johnson; The Buffalo Bunch; and de Homem-Christo's brother, Paul de Homem-Christo, who goes by the name Play Paul. (Selections from Crydamoure's roster of singles were made available on two compilation CDs, *Waves* and *Waves II.*)

Outside of Crydamoure, de Homem-Christo produced Sébastien Tellier's album, *Sexuality*, in 2008. Two years later, he co-produced Kavinsky's *Nightcall* EP with SebastiAn, a French musician and DJ affiliated with Ed Banger Records. Additionally, in 2012, de Homem-Christo was featured on Tellier's album *My God Is Blue*, co-writing the track "My Poseidon."

Although Bangalter and de Homem-Christo seemed to wind down both Roulé and Crydamoure as they prepared to work on Daft Punk's third studio album *Human After All* in 2003, there continues to be speculation that more music may be on the way from their long-dormant labels. This is particularly true since Roulé is said to have begun quietly reissuing several of its twelve-inch vinyls in November 2012. As DJ Falcon has said of Bangalter, "You never know what to expect from Thomas."

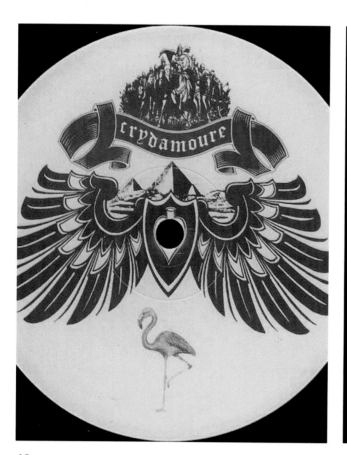

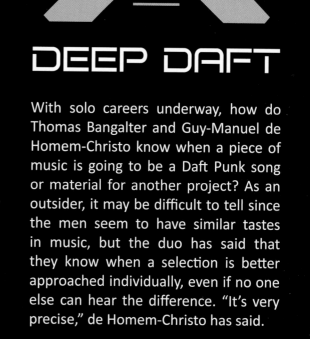

DEEP DAFT

With solo careers underway, how do Thomas Bangalter and Guy-Manuel de Homem-Christo know when a piece of music is going to be a Daft Punk song or material for another project? As an outsider, it may be difficult to tell since the men seem to have similar tastes in music, but the duo has said that they know when a selection is better approached individually, even if no one else can hear the difference. "It's very precise," de Homem-Christo has said.

CRYDAMOURE DISCOGRAPHY

Year	Title	Artist
1997	"Santa Claus"/"Holiday On Ice"	Le Knight Club
1997	"White Winds"/"Santa Claus (remix)"	Paul Johnson/Le Knight Club
1998	"Troobadoor"/"Mirage"	Le Knight Club
1998	"Intergalactik Disko"	Le Knight Club vs DJ Sneak
1999	"Boogie Shell"/"Coco Girlz"/"Mosquito"/"Coral Twist"	Le Knight Club
1999	"T.I.T.T.S. (Take It To The Street)"/"Music Box"	The Buffalo Bunch
1999	"Hysteria"	Le Knight Club
1999	"Lovers"	Raw Man
1999	"United Tastes of Deelat"	Deelat
2000	"Spaced Out"/"Holy Ghostz"	Play Paul
2000	"Wrath of Zeus"	Eternals
2000	"The Turkish Avenger"/"Feel Inside"	Sedat
2000	*Waves* (compilation album)	Le Knight Club
2001	"Gator"/"Chérie D'Amoure"	Le Knight Club
2001	"Mad Joe"/"In Flight"	Archigram
2002	"Soul Bells"/"Palm Beat"/"Tropicall"	Le Knight Club
2002	"Nymphae Song"/"Rhumba"	Le Knight Club
2002	"Carnaval"	Archigram
2002	"If You Give Me The Love I Want"/"Playground"/"Loaded"	Crydajam
2003	"Doggystyle"	Archigram
2003	*Waves II* (compilation album)	Archigram

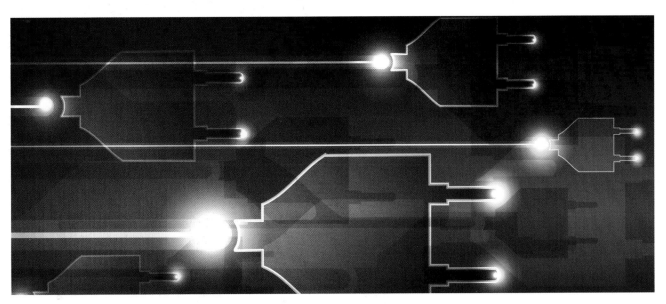

DISCOVERY

SWAPPING PINK thread detailing for a puddle of shimmery silver, Daft Punk's logo is emblazoned, once again, on the duo's second studio album. The tonal change is both ornamental and substantive for the French duo, as *Discovery* steers fans away from the patchy roughness of *Homework* to a smoothly produced, pop-prone track-list that, at times, can be as easy on the ears as it is on one's dancing feet.

A sophomore effort—whether by a band, film director, or an author—can often be more of the same, a "safe" endeavor that harnesses and capitalizes on the techniques or elements that got the artist noticed in the first place. Daft Punk's *Discovery* was nothing of the sort.

Daft Punk's visual playfulness came to the fore with the *Discovery* release.

Instead, Thomas Bangalter and Guy-Manuel de Homem-Christo changed up their successful formula with their second album (released in March 2001 by Virgin Records), and embraced a broader range of pop, funk, and progressive rock, eschewing dance music's conventional benchmarks in an effort to reinvent themselves. This was just the first of many reinventions throughout their career thus far.

The heavy emphasis on filtered disco samples, phase-shifted textures, and 909 drum beats mostly based around loops and grooves that had become hallmarks of modern house (a sound Daft Punk helped to define) took a backseat to traditionally styled songs with distinctive rock overtones and body-popping electro beats reminiscent of the late 70s and early 80s. If *Homework* had been an effort to show rock fans that electronic music was cool, *Discovery*, conversely, told the electronic kids that rock and roll is here to stay.

Rather than produce a tribute album devoted to the music of their childhood, Daft Punk instead wanted to focus on their relationship—honest, playful, and fun—with the music of the period, including disco, electro, rock, heavy metal, and classical tunes. Electronic dance music had shown that it was possible to destroy the rules when making music but, in doing so, the genre had established new rules of its own. Daft Punk set out to shatter those in order to create songs in the *spirit* of house music rather than the *style*. Bangalter has said that one of the cool things about the house music spirit—and the same can be said for that of hip-hop—is that it inspires musicians to use instruments for things they weren't designed for, and to veer away from the instruction manual.

On *Discovery,* there are guitars that sound like synthesizers and synthesizers that sound like guitars. The recording studio—again, Bangalter's bedroom (although the duo also did some recording in New Jersey and other places)—was stocked with lots of gear, including guitars,

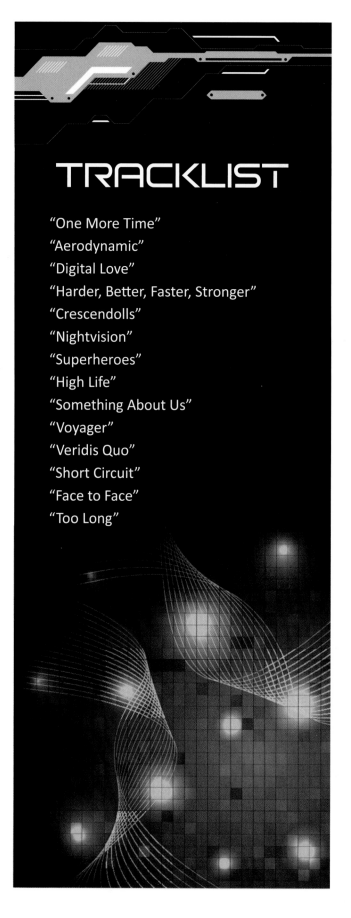

TRACKLIST

"One More Time"
"Aerodynamic"
"Digital Love"
"Harder, Better, Faster, Stronger"
"Crescendolls"
"Nightvision"
"Superheroes"
"High Life"
"Something About Us"
"Voyager"
"Veridis Quo"
"Short Circuit"
"Face to Face"
"Too Long"

Homework	Discovery
Showing rock kids that dance music is cool	Showing dance music kids that rock is cool
Heavy reliance on sampling	Only four samples used/"fake samples"
Minimal vocals	Greater emphasis on vocals/collaboration
Traditional house	Rock, disco, synth-pop-inspired house
Low-tech sound	High-tech sound
Programming instruments	Playing instruments
Loops and grooves	Traditional-style songs, featuring instrument solos
Repetition	Variation
Machine-like quality to music	More human approach to music
Album promoted as camera-shy, occasionally masked humans	Album promoted as full-fledged robots

bass guitars, keyboards, effects pedals, and drum machines to produce complex, meticulous tracks; reportedly, every track on *Discovery* used a different phase shifter and vocoder effect. Daft Punk played and sampled their own instruments (de Homem-Christo was usually on guitar, with Bangalter on keyboard and bass, although they both play all three instruments) and went out of their way to use instruments in ways they weren't intended to be used. The benefit of working in a home studio was that the musicians could take all the time they needed to experiment without watching the clock. Many times, stretches of music were sampled and re-sampled; de Homem-Christo has estimated that half of the sampled material on *Discovery* was originally played live. (Some of the duo's reported samples are not samples at all, but newly recorded elements that sounded like "fake samples," such as the instrumental "Nightvision," which is a dead-ringer for 10cc's "I'm Not in Love.")

Discovery was ultimately a multimillion-selling album and, in 2012, *Rolling Stone* named it the eighth greatest EDM album of all time. It kicks off with the perky party tune "One More Time," featuring DJ, producer, and singer Romanthony's heavily processed vocals (he also penned the lyrics, co-produced, and sang on the album's final track "Too Long"). Until the release of "Get Lucky" in April 2013, "One More Time" was Daft Punk's highest-charting song, peaking at number two on the UK Singles Chart in 2000; it was also one of the duo's few charting songs in the United States, climbing to number sixty-one on the *Billboard* Hot 100 (additionally, *Mixmag* readers voted it as the greatest dance record of all time in February 2013).

The instrumental track "Aerodynamic" starts off with a funky groove that segues into a metallic solo on electric guitar—an unlikely facet for a dance record—and then fuses them together in a space-age combo. "Digital Love" also features a guitar-sounding solo and offers an electronic pop song vibe; it features one of only four samples on *Discovery* ("I Love You More" by George

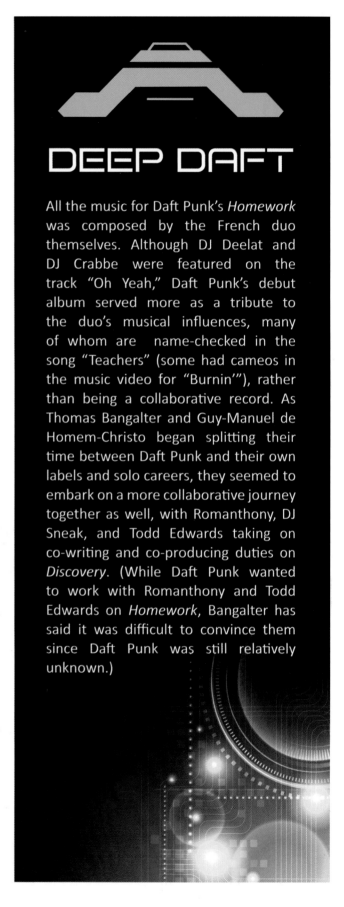

DEEP DAFT

All the music for Daft Punk's *Homework* was composed by the French duo themselves. Although DJ Deelat and DJ Crabbe were featured on the track "Oh Yeah," Daft Punk's debut album served more as a tribute to the duo's musical influences, many of whom are name-checked in the song "Teachers" (some had cameos in the music video for "Burnin'"), rather than being a collaborative record. As Thomas Bangalter and Guy-Manuel de Homem-Christo began splitting their time between Daft Punk and their own labels and solo careers, they seemed to embark on a more collaborative journey together as well, with Romanthony, DJ Sneak, and Todd Edwards taking on co-writing and co-producing duties on *Discovery*. (While Daft Punk wanted to work with Romanthony and Todd Edwards on *Homework*, Bangalter has said it was difficult to convince them since Daft Punk was still relatively unknown.)

Little Anthony and the Imperials: Daft Punk sampled widely varied eras on *Discovery*.

DEEP DAFT

Four samples were used on *Discovery*:

- George Duke's "I Love You More" on "Digital Love"
- Edwin Birdson's "Cola Bottle Baby" on "Harder, Better, Faster, Stronger"
- "Can You Imagine" by The Imperials on "Crescendolls"
- Barry Manilow's "Who's Been Sleeping in My Bed" on "Superheroes"

This time around, rather than simply creating new music from samples (Guy-Manuel de Homem-Christo has said that Daft Punk comes across "maybe one good sample every six months or so"), Daft Punk reworked (or emulated) them, adding instrumental and vocal performances. The duo plays virtually all of the instruments on *Discovery*; because the instruments are not always used for their intended purpose, the result is a lot of effects and distortions, and they are not always easily recognizable.

Duke), and has a Supertramp-esque bridge (Daft Punk used the original Wurlitzer piano the group used). With lyrics about unspoken love written by DJ Sneak and performed by Daft Punk, the song features a prominent keyboard solo, aided by music sequencers in its second half.

"Harder, Better, Faster, Stronger," which won the Grammy Award for Best Dance Recording in 2009, features Daft Punk's signature robotic vocal performance. "Superheroes" opens with a drumroll and features classical arpeggios in the vein of Queen's music for the film *Flash Gordon* (it also samples Barry Manilow's "Who's Been Sleeping in My Bed") and a pounding four-on-the-floor drive. "Face to Face," featuring vocals by producer Todd Edwards (who also wrote the lyrics and co-produced the song), reached #1 on the *Billboard* dance chart in 2004. All of the tracks for *Discovery* provide the soundtrack for the film *Interstella 5555: The 5tory of the 5ecret 5tar 5ystem.*

DEEP DAFT

The late Anthony Moore, better known as Romanthony, was a DJ, producer, and singer whose work crossed several genres, including house, R&B, and hip-hop. Long-standing admirers of Romanthony's work (he was one of Daft Punk's many influences mentioned on *Homework's* "Teachers"), Daft Punk met him at the 1996 Winter Music Conference in Miami, and they became friends. Bangalter has said that the duo invited him to sing on *Discovery* because they thought he made "emotional music," and when Romanthony agreed, it made them "very happy."

Reportedly, every track on the *Discovery* album used a vocoder effect of some kind.

A ROBOT IS BORN

Although Daft Punk wore masks or covered their faces in publicity shots during the *Homework* era, it wasn't until *Discovery* that they unveiled the first installment of their trademark robot personas, which came with a backstory of their own. As the story goes, at 9:09 A.M. on September 9, 1999 (as Daft Punk was working on the *Discovery* album) there was "a little accident," as Bangalter has called it, with the machinery in the studio. Having to seek medical attention as well as some reconstructive surgery, Daft Punk reemerged looking like robots. (Although they have forgotten aspects of their life before the accident, luckily most of the recording and final production of the album was already complete.) With a "new chip" in their brains, coupled with their beating human hearts, Daft Punk would now focus attention—for the promotion of *Discovery* and beyond—on the music rather than the men, which is where they've always firmly believed it belongs.

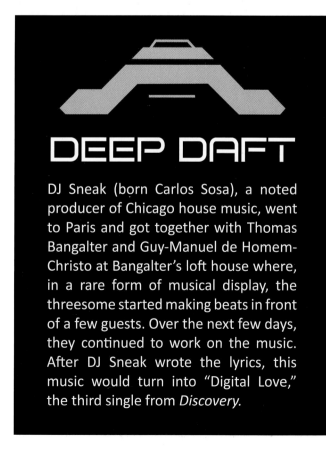

DEEP DAFT

DJ Sneak (born Carlos Sosa), a noted producer of Chicago house music, went to Paris and got together with Thomas Bangalter and Guy-Manuel de Homem-Christo at Bangalter's loft house where, in a rare form of musical display, the threesome started making beats in front of a few guests. Over the next few days, they continued to work on the music. After DJ Sneak wrote the lyrics, this music would turn into "Digital Love," the third single from *Discovery*.

Daft Punk's newly unveiled helmets would become a mainstay of their career.

INTERSTELLA 5555: THE 5TORY OF THE 5ECRET 5TAR 5YSTEM

Daft Punk set their first film deep in outer space.

For Thomas Bangalter and Guy-Manuel de Homem-Christo, creative achievement has never been just about the music. Since their early days of experimenting with drum machines and beat boxes in their bedrooms, they wanted to take a sweeping approach to their art that would incorporate things like their love of cinema, character, and having fun into everything from their album covers to their personas. Rather than marketing ploys, Bangalter has called these satellite endeavors part of the "general universe" in which Daft Punk creates.

Certainly, by the early aughts, Daft Punk came to be known as more than just purveyors of music, particularly after the popular music videos for the

first studio album, *Homework*, helped form the duo's brand. However, arguably, it wasn't until their first film, *Interstella 5555: The 5tory of the 5ecret 5tar 5ystem*, that it became clear that music was just one piece of Daft Punk's mysterious puzzle.

The idea for *Interstella* came during an early *Discovery* recording session, and Daft Punk further developed the concept with collaborator Cédric Hervet. The three brought the album and completed story to Tokyo, hoping to create the film with Leiji Matsumoto, a well-known creator of several anime and manga series, as well as a childhood hero of Daft Punk's. Matsumoto agreed to come onboard as visual supervisor, and Kazuhisa Takenouchi directed the film.

Production began in October 2000 and ended in April 2003; the film is said to have cost $4 million. Released in December 2003 (the first four episodes of the film were shown on MTV and Cartoon Network in 2001), *Interstella 5555: The 5tory of the 5ecret 5tar 5ystem* is a sixty-eight-minute feature-length film about the intergalactic abduction of an extraterrestrial pop band. It has no dialogue—without the barrier of language, Bangalter has said, everyone is able to participate in the fantasy—and utilizes all fourteen tracks from the second studio album *Discovery*, which, when played one after the other in order, sync perfectly with each episode of the film.

Japanese cartoonist and animator Leiji Matsumoto at the 70th annual Venice International Film Festival, in Venice, Italy, in 2013.

SOUNDTRACK: "ONE MORE TIME"

An extraterrestrial pop band featuring four blue-skinned music stars—Stella, bass player; Arpegius, guitarist; Baryl, drummer; and Octave, keyboardist and vocalist—are performing the song "One More Time," the first track on *Discovery,* to a similarly blue-skinned audience on an alien planet.

The characters in *Interstella 5555* travel to and from distant planets.

SOUNDTRACK: "AERODYNAMIC"

A team of humanoid troops storm the arena. They subdue the band and the audience with gas, carting the four musicians onto a large spaceship.

SOUNDTRACK: "DIGITAL LOVE"

Floating nearby in space, a lone blue spaceman named Shep (whose ship is shaped like an electric guitar) is daydreaming about Stella, the bass player of the kidnapped band, just as a typical teenager fantasizes about rock bands and romantic love. He receives a distress signal about the abduction and becomes determined to save the band, rocketing off in pursuit of the kidnappers. It is his chance to become the hero and save the girl—and the music. He chases the kidnapped vessel through space and onto Earth, where the kidnappers land and deboard with the band members (who are unconscious and under some kind of spell) while

a creepy white-haired man, the Earl of Darkwood, watches. (After all, every hero story needs a bad guy.) Meanwhile, Shep and his ship make a hard landing in a dense forest.

SOUNDTRACK: "HARDER, BETTER, FASTER, STRONGER"

Taken to a large underground facility, the interstellar band members are stripped of their clothing, have their skin painted and their memories rewritten (their old memories are stored on disks), are re-dressed to resemble humans, and are implanted with mind-control devices that are hidden behind sunglasses.

SOUNDTRACK: "THE CRESCENDOLLS"

The Earl de Darkwood turns out to be the ringleader of the abduction. Posing as the band's manager, he takes the band members to a recording studio and secures them a record deal as The Crescendolls. The band releases a single titled "One More Time," which races up the charts, rocketing The Crescendolls to worldwide fame (they are shown signing autographs and appearing on magazine covers).

SOUNDTRACK: "NIGHTVISION"

As the band is forced to endure a rigorous schedule, a cloaked Shep walks the streets, spies the band's photos and videos up in lights, and discovers what has happened.

SOUNDTRACK: "SUPERHEROES"

While the band is performing a concert, Shep rockets into the stadium, fires a hand-held beam device, and is able to free all of the band members except his crush, Stella, from the effects of the mind-control sunglasses. Forced to leave Stella behind, Shep and the other band members hijack a van and escape, but during a chase the Earl de Darkwood's henchmen mortally wound Shep before crashing their vehicle.

SOUNDTRACK: "HIGH LIFE"

Meanwhile, Stella, still under the control of the Earl, is taken to a fashion show. Just before leaving for another event, she picks up a card the Earl accidentally drops that says, "Darkwood Manor 05/05 5:55"—the first reference to the numeric

film title, *Interstella 5555: The 5tory of the 5ecret 5tar 5ystem*. She slips it into her clothing. Later, she is taken to a Gold Record Award ceremony, where The Crescendolls have received a nomination (along with an animated Daft Punk, seen sitting in the audience). When the Gold Record is awarded to The Crescendolls (one wonders whether Daft Punk is suggesting something here about the nature of the award shows since it is a robot-like, mind-controlled band that has won) and Stella takes the stage, Baryl, who is hiding in the audience, uses the beam device to snap Stella out of her trance, and the two enter a waiting taxicab driven by Octave to escape.

SOUNDTRACK: "SOMETHING ABOUT US"

The reunited band members gather around Shep, who is dying. Shep reaches for Stella, and the two experience a dream-like sequence that's similar to Shep's earlier daydream. Shep reveals the band's true identity to them.

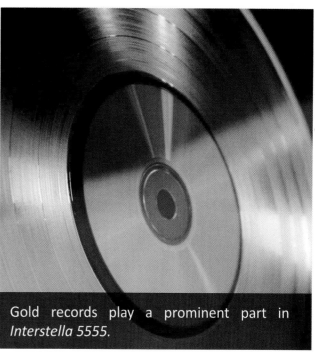

Gold records play a prominent part in *Interstella 5555*.

Shep's spirit shoots into the sky after his death.

SOUNDTRACK: "VOYAGER"

The band drives out of the city to bury Shep by the roots of a large tree atop a cliff and to pay tribute to his spirit, which emerges from the ground and shoots up into the night sky. As the band is driving away, they screech to a halt and double back to a road sign that says "Darkwood Manor"—the same name that appeared on the card Stella found. The band drives off in the direction of Darkwood Manor.

SOUNDTRACK: "VERIDIS QUO"

The band members reach a dark, mysterious castle and, once inside, find a journal titled *Veridis Quo* inside of a secret chamber. The journal gets the band—and the viewer—up to speed on what the Earl de Darkwood has been up to. For many years, he has used aliens to make music that is worthy of a Gold Record; when he has claimed 5,555 Gold Records, he will amass a great power that will

allow him to rule the universe (The Crescendolls were awarded Gold Record number 5,555).

Suddenly, the band members are surrounded by the Earl's henchmen, who bring them to an underground cavern where Earl grabs Stella and puts her into a big machine that's lined with his Gold Records, intent on offering her as a sacrifice. The next scene borrows its climax and dramatic fight sequence from a typical Hollywood action film. The other band members free themselves from the guards, and Arpegius rushes to the Earl before he unleashes his power, which causes the last Gold Record to fall from his hands into an abyss. When the Earl tries to reach for it, he, too, falls in and presumably dies. Next, Arpegius rescues Stella from the device, Octave takes the mysterious *Veridis Quo* journal, and the band flees the castle, which begins to self-destruct. As in Hollywood, the good guys make it out in the nick of time.

SOUNDTRACK: "SHORT CIRCUIT"

Now that they're aware of the Earl de Darkwood's evil scheme, the band travels back to the record company. On the way, Octave finds a photo of the memory disks on a page from the *Veridis Quo* journal—he removes the page and puts it in his jacket pocket. When they arrive at the record company building, Octave breaks in, gets past the security guards—who are watching a soccer match between France and Japan, representing the collaboration of Daft Punk and Matsumoto—and finds the master recording of "One More Time," under which are the band's archived memory disks (the concept of a memory disk would be explored again by Daft Punk on the 2013 studio album *Random Access Memories*). Octave suddenly finds himself surrounded by guards, and when he reaches into his jacket for the page of *Veridis Quo*, they mistake it for a weapon. They tase him and he falls to the ground, his skin returning to its original blue color. Surprised, the record company exec who signed the band takes the page from Octave's hand, realizing what the disks really are.

SOUNDTRACK: "FACE TO FACE"

A news report shows the world what has happened to The Crescendolls—how they were not the only musical group to have been kidnapped by the Earl de Darkwood and how there are plans to send them back home. Construction crews unearth Shep's ship as the police investigate. Octave wakes up and is greeted by the band members, whose blue skin and memories have been restored. As the band prepares to leave Earth, throngs of well-wishers gather to bid them farewell, and their launch is televised all over the world.

SOUNDTRACK: "TOO LONG"

As the band's spaceship heads toward home, the Earl's essence appears and attacks the ship, but is defeated by Shep's essence (a statue of Shep will later be erected on his home planet), and the band makes it home. As the band members once again take the stage, the audience dances, as does everyone on Earth who is watching the performance on television screens.

The camera zooms out of the celebration, taking the viewer away from the concert, the alien planet, and the star cluster, and onto a record player where the vinyl record of Daft Punk's *Discovery* is spinning in a child's bedroom that's filled with Daft Punk memorabilia and other toys. Nearby, a little boy has fallen asleep on a floor pillow surrounded by toy versions of The Crescendolls and Shep's spaceship (the Earl de Darkwood and his henchmen are tucked away in a toy chest). Presumably, the entire film is revealed to be a figment of the boy's imagination, a theme that was also present on Daft Punk's first album *Homework*, which was recorded in Bangalter's bedroom and the artwork of which features scenes from a bedroom. The boy is tucked into bed, and the needle is removed from the record, bringing both its play, and the movie, to an end.

DAFT CLUB

Daft Club, a remix album released by Virgin Records in CD format in 2003, was initially intended as a promotional vehicle for Daft Punk's second album, *Discovery*; its songs were made available for free to those who bought early versions of *Discovery* through Daft Punk's online music service of the same name in 2001.

Daft Club featured all of the tracks from *Discovery* with the exception of five ("Nightvision," "Superheroes," "High Life," "Veridis Quo," and "Short Circuit"), all of which were remixed by a variety of Daft Punk's favorite artists, such as British electronic dance duo Basement Jaxx, production team The Neptunes (featuring *Random Access Memories* collaborator Pharrell Williams), Gonzales (another *RAM* associate), and DJ/producer Laidback Luke.

The album also included additional remixes of "Face to Face," "Harder, Better, Faster, Stronger," *Discovery*'s second single "Aerodynamic" (as well as its B-side, "Aerodynamite"), the previously unreleased track "Ouverture," and a remix of "Phoenix," the only track included from Daft Punk's first album, *Homework*.

Pharrell Williams, shown on stage in a yellow cap, contributes a remix to *Daft Club* as part of The Neptunes.

DIGITAL DOWNLOAD (2001)

"Ouverture"

"Aerodynamic" (special edition remix)

"Phoenix (Basement Jaxx Remix)"

"One More Time (Romanthony's Unplugged 'A Capella')"

"Aerodynamic (Slum Village Remix)"

"Digital Love (Club Mix by Boris Dlugosch)"

"Alive 1997" ("Daftendirektour and Live Birmingham 1997")

"Harder, Better, Faster, Stronger" (instrumental)

"Harder, Better, Faster, Stronger" (a capella)

"Harder, Better, Faster, Stronger (Jess & Crabbe Regulator Mix)"

"Harder, Better, Faster, Stronger (The Neptunes Instrumental)"

"Crescendolls (Laidback Luke Remix)"

"Face to Face (Demon Remix)"

COMPACT DISC (2003)

"Ouverture"

"Aerodynamic (Daft Punk Remix)"

"Harder, Better, Faster, Stronger (The Neptunes Remix)"

"Face to Face (Cosmo Vitelli Remix)"

"Phoenix (Basement Jaxx Remix)"

"Digital Love (Boris Dlugosch Remix)"

"Harder, Better, Faster, Stronger (Jess & Crabbe Remix)"

"Face to Face (Demon Remix)"

"Crescendolls (Laidback Luke Remix)"

"Aerodynamic (Slum Village Remix)"

"Too Long (Gonzales Version)"

"Aerodynamite"

"One More Time (Romanthony's Unplugged)"

"Something About Us (Love Theme from *Interstella 5555*)"

Japan bonus track:

"Voyager (Dominique Torti's Wild Style Edit)"

DEEP DAFT

Limited edition copies of the film *Interstella 5555: The 5tory of the 5ecret 5tar 5ystem* featured *Daft Club* as a second disk, although the track "Something About Us"—the love theme of the film—is omitted from this version. A limited edition of the album was also released in Japan and included an extra track, "Voyager (Dominique Torti's Wild Style Edit)," and a bonus DVD/video that contained a preview of *Interstella 5555*, interviews with Daft Punk, the music video for "Crescendolls," and a video montage for "Something About Us" that included assorted film scenes.

HUMAN AFTER ALL

DAFT PUNK takes aim at the media with their third studio album, whose cover features the duo's familiar logo, but this time inside a television screen. Although not quite unplugged, *Human After All* offers a minimalist Daft Punk, which strays from the customary party vibe for a deeper, darker, and more subtle offering.

In March 2005, Daft Punk released its highly anticipated third studio album, *Human After All*, a minimalist, less pop-oriented record with hard-edged, low-res electronic dance numbers that aimed to reinvent the duo once again.

This time around, Thomas Bangalter and Guy-Manuel de Homem-Christo set a new kind of parameter for themselves: Rather than experimenting musically—as they'd done to create the relentless pulse of *Homework* and the lush, expansive *Discovery*—they decided to produce *Human After All* within a limited time frame and with a limited kit. Whereas Daft Punk's other studio albums were years in the making, *Human After All* was created in about six weeks (Bangalter and de Homem-Christo spent only ten days in their recording studio) primarily using two drum machines, two guitars, one vocoder, and one eight-track machine. Bangalter has said that he and de Homem-Christo were "seduced" by the idea of doing a counterpoint to *Discovery*, and deliberately created an unpolished record in their continuing quest to address the relationship between humanity and technology. Although the album premiered at #1 on *Billboard*'s Top Electronic Albums listing, its roughness—like "a stone that's unworked," Bangalter has said—wound up alienating some fans who believed the album was repetitive and unremarkable. ("Sometimes we feel appreciated and sometimes we don't," Bangalter has said.) Whereas a playfulness had come to embody Daft Punk's work, as it did the genre of electronic dance itself, *Human After All* seemed darker than its predecessors, inspired by the oppressive world of George Orwell's seminal novel *1984*. Although the album received mixed reviews, audiences responded favorably to the tracks when they were played in Daft Punk's Alive 2006/2007 tour.

Bangalter and de Homem-Christo did virtually no publicity in support of *Human After All,* refusing interview requests. The artwork for the Japanese edition of the album featured the following quote:

"We believe that *Human After All* speaks for itself." Although de Homem-Christo would later say that decision was one of the biggest marketing mistakes Daft Punk has ever made, at the time the duo felt it was illogical to chat with the press when the album itself was a commentary on the overwhelming presence that television and media had become

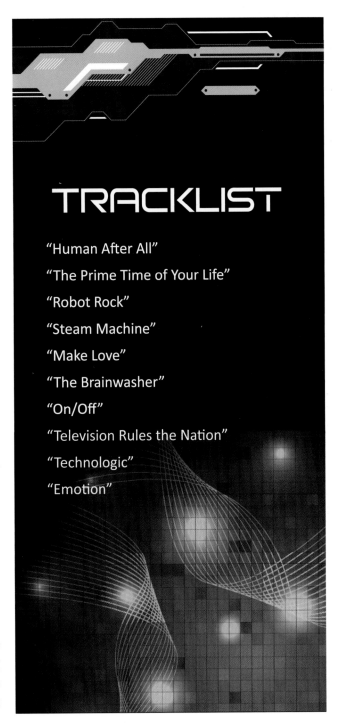

TRACKLIST

"Human After All"

"The Prime Time of Your Life"

"Robot Rock"

"Steam Machine"

"Make Love"

"The Brainwasher"

"On/Off"

"Television Rules the Nation"

"Technologic"

"Emotion"

George Orwell's *1984* has informed everything from Apple Computer's Super Bowl Macintosh ad to Daft Punk's explorations of humanity and technology. Like the futuristic dystopian novel, *Human After All* plays with the image of the omnipresent telescreen and invokes themes such as psychological manipulation and information control, venturing into the place where there is no darkness, or, perhaps a first for a Daft Punk studio album, to a place where there is.

Discovery	Human After All
Two and a half years in the making	Made in six weeks
High production value	Minimalist, stripped-down feel
Lush instrumental palette	Primarily recorded using two drum machines, two guitars, one vocoder, and one eight-track machine
Sleek	Unpolished
Feel-good record	Inspired by George Orwell's *1984*

in day-to-day living. *Human After All*'s album cover displayed Daft Punk's logo planted firmly within the confines of a television screen. Similarly, each of the four tracks released as singles ("Robot Rock," "Technologic," "Human After All," and "The Prime Time of Your Life") featured various cover images in the same fashion. The accompanying music videos for each single all began with the words "special presentation" in 70s, made-for-TV-style graphics and revolved around a television theme. (Television is also directly referenced in the titles of the songs "On/Off" and "Television Rules the Nation.")

The album's first single, "Robot Rock," samples the Breakwater song "Release the Beast" from the 1980 album *Splashdown,* giving the track a prominent synthesizer riff that's emulated by the duo on electric guitar. The music video, directed by Daft Punk (who also directed the "Fresh" video from the *Homework* album), features Bangalter and de Homem-Christo performing on a stage in front of bright television screens and under flashing stage lights, with Bangalter playing a double-neck guitar and de Homem-Christo on drums. It is the first of their videos to exclusively feature the duo.

The second single, "Technologic," is known for its vocoded voice chants of technological commands that flash on a television monitor and are spoken in rhythm (the word "it" occurs 350 times). The third music video to be directed by Daft Punk, "Technologic" stars a little robot whose little red pyramid became the inspiration for the duo's wildly successful Alive 2006/2007 tour. The album's third single, "Human After All," was the only song released without an accompanying music video. Although the duo set out to make one, the venture turned into the full-length feature *Daft Punk's Electroma.*

The fourth and final single, "The Prime Time of Your Life," featured a music video that was released as part of the Daft Punk anthology, *Musique Vol. 1 1993–2005.* It was directed by

special-effects mastermind Tony Gardner, who has worked on many films, including *Shallow Hal, The Addams Family,* and *127 Hours*, as well as Michael Jackson's *Thriller* video. Gardner, who is responsible for the makeup effects of the popular GEICO cavemen characters, also headed up the design of the robot in Daft Punk's "Technologic" video and helped out with special effects and prosthetics for *Daft Punk's Electroma* (see page 66).

"The Prime Time of Your Life" is a dark video that, of all the tracks and videos associated with *Human After All*, perhaps best portrays the album's commentary on media, particularly because it focuses on children. It opens with a skull moving its jaw, then zooms out to reveal that the skull is merely a reflection in the eye of a young girl who is watching late night television from her bed. On the television screen, everyone—from marketers on a home shopping channel to the weatherman—appears as living skeletons (Daft Punk makes a

RANDOM MEMORY

"When we put out *Human After All,* I got a lot of bad feedback, like, 'It's so repetitive. There's nothing new. Daft Punk used to be good.' Then they came back with the light show, and everyone shut their mouths. They said, '*Ooh la-la!*' People even apologized, like, 'How could we have misjudged Daft Punk?' The live show changed everything."

—Pedro Winter, Daft Punk manager (1996 to 2008), to *Paper* magazine in 2007

cameo appearance as skeletons during a news segment). The young girl turns off the TV and walks over to her dresser to look at the photo frames on her bureau. Although she appears human in all the photos, the other individuals are all living skeletons (one photo, in particular, triggers a flashback to a time when she received a necklace while at the beach).

The girl goes into the bathroom, where she is seen in the mirror with a skeletal rendition of Britney Spears (a reference to the cover of Spears's 2004 album, *Greatest Hits: My Prerogative*). The girl takes off her necklace, lays it on the sink, and opens a drawer, extracting a razor blade. She slits her right hand with the blade and, with her other hand, pulls the skin off her right hand. She continues to cut and tear off her skin until her head, torso, and arms are skinless. She stares at herself in the mirror, and then, after a series of

flashbacks, faints. The girl's parents, who do not appear as skeletons, find their daughter lying on the bathroom floor. As they rush to her side, the

When it was leaked online several months prior to its official release, *Human After All,* with its stripped-down sound, was believed to be a fake album intended to foil digital piracy.

camera pans back to the photo frames, where all of the people in the photos now appear as humans rather than skeletons, as they were originally shown. In the video's final scene, the young girl, now a skeleton, is on television waving at two young skeletons who are holding a jump rope.

A limited pressing of 3,000 copies of the album *Human After All: Remixes* was released exclusively for Japan in March 2006 (although many of the remixes were incorporated into the Alive 2006/2007 tour), and featured remixes previously unavailable on CD. A limited edition of the album also included a set of Daft Punk Kubricks, block-style figurines.

TRACKLIST

"Robot Rock (Soulwax Remix)"

"Human After All (SebastiAn Remix)"

"Technologic (Peaches No Logic Remix)"

"The Brainwasher (Erol Alkan's Horrorhouse Dub)"

"The Prime Time of Your Life (Para One Remix)"

"Human After All ('Guy-Man After All' Justice Remix)"

"Technologic (Digitalism's Highway to Paris Remix)"

"Human After All (Alter Ego Remix)"

"Technologic (Vitalic Remix)"

"Robot Rock (Daft Punk Maximum Overdrive Mix)"

In 2009, ten influential music blogs banded together to produce an unofficial remix album, titled Remix After All, in response to the official remix album's limited availability and because it failed to cover all ten of the Human After All tracks. Each blog chose one track from the album and appointed its own producer to create the remix. On May 19, one day before the remix album's release, each blog exclusively pre-released its own mix as a low-quality promotional MP3. The following day, the remix album in its entirety was made available for free download with full-quality MP3s.

TRACKLIST

"Human After All (The Disco Villains Remix)"

"The Prime Time of Your Life (Tits & Clits Remix)"

"Robot Rock (Immuzikation Remix)"

"Steam Machine (The Company Kang Remix)"

"Make Love (Chew Fu and Substantial Small Room Sax Fix)"

"The Brainwasher (Melee Beats Remix)"

"On/Off (The Noizy Kidz Daft Zapping Remix)"

"Television Rules the Nation (Dirty Disco Youth Remix)"

"Technologic (Kids at the Bar Remix)"

"Emotion (Werewolf by Night Remix)"

ELECTROMA

A funny thing happened on the way to making the video for Daft Punk's "Human After All," the single from the studio album of the same name: the duo made a movie instead.

Daft Punk's Electroma, the 2006 art-house film, became the first full-length feature directorial pursuit for the French duo who, until this point, had only directed music videos for their singles, "Fresh," "Robot Rock," and "Technologic." Although the seventy-four-minute film was totally unplanned and represented new ground for the groundbreaking-inclined pair, the venture felt natural for Thomas Bangalter and Guy-Manuel de Homem-Christo. They undertook the effort with the same philosophy that they do all of

The American West, as seen in Electroma.

their artistic endeavors: Create without rules and without standards, and when approaching something unfamiliar, learn from scratch. While Daft Punk's earlier long-form cinematic ventures—*D.A.F.T.: A Story About Dogs, Androids, Firemen and Tomatoes* and *Interstella 5555: The 5tory of the 5ecret 5tar 5ystem*—were made to complement studio albums, *Electroma* is the first that does not feature Daft Punk's music. Instead, the soundtrack includes works by Todd Rundgren, Brian Eno, Sébastien Tellier, Curtis Mayfield, and others.

Wholly without dialogue, *Electroma* is an experimental film (Bangalter has said it "does not require your brain to function") that was shot on 35mm Kodak stock under the cinematography direction of Bangalter—who read more than 200 back issues of *American Cinematographer* for the job—in eleven days, mostly in California. (Many of the scenes take place in Inyo County along U.S. Route 395, and in the town of Independence.)

The film follows the quest of two robots, credited as Hero Robot #1 and Hero Robot #2, who represent the Daft Punk band members, wearing the duo's signature jackets and silver and gold helmets. The roles are played by Peter Hurteau and Michael Reich, production assistants (and "two really cool kids," Bangalter has said) for Daft Punk's production company Daft Arts. The inexperienced actors were also chosen for their size and physique—they fit into the leather outfits and robot helmets that

fashion designer Hedi Slimane designed specifically for Daft Punk in 2004.

As the film opens, the robot-heroes emerge out of a vast southwestern U.S. landscape and get into a 1987 Ferrari 412 that displays a vanity license plate that reads "HUMAN." They drive through what appears to be a typical American town, although the residents all wear the same gold and silver robot helmets as they perform everyday activities, such as playing at a local park, mowing lawns, and attending a church wedding. Soon, the robot-

heroes arrive at a facility, which is shown in stark black and white imagery, where tech people pour liquid latex over their heads, forming grotesque human-like faces (the work of makeup mastermind Tony Gardner) that call to mind Charles the dog-faced human from Daft Punk's "Da Funk" and "Fresh" music videos.

With their new human heads, the two men leave the facility and strut Tony Manero–like down the road, outfitted in handyman-type overalls (which happen to be white, the same color as

John Travolta's famous suit in *Saturday Night Fever*) that cover their black leather jackets. The townspeople, apparently appalled by the robot-heroes' transformation, stop, stare, and soon form an angry—albeit expressionless—mob, forcing the heroes (whose faces have begun to melt in the sun) to take cover in a public restroom. Inside, the gold-helmeted robot tears off his ruined latex head and throws it into the toilet, encouraging his silver-helmeted companion, who seems more saddened and upset, to do the same, and they emerge from the public restroom as their original robot selves. They begin to walk—and walk—across the desert until, eventually, the silver-helmeted robot-hero stops, removes his jacket,

and turns around to reveal a switch on his back. His companion flips the switch, which begins a countdown, and the silver robot walks away until, when the timer reaches zero, he is blown apart.

The gold robot-hero surveys the pieces of his companion, gathers them into a pile, and continues to walk, this time alone. Eventually, he falls to his knees, takes off his own jacket, and tries to reach the switch on his back in an attempt to self-destruct. Perhaps Daft Punk is suggesting that in a partnership—be it a friendship, a marriage, or an electronic music duo—one cannot survive without the other, nor would one want to. However, he can't reach the switch on his own, so he removes

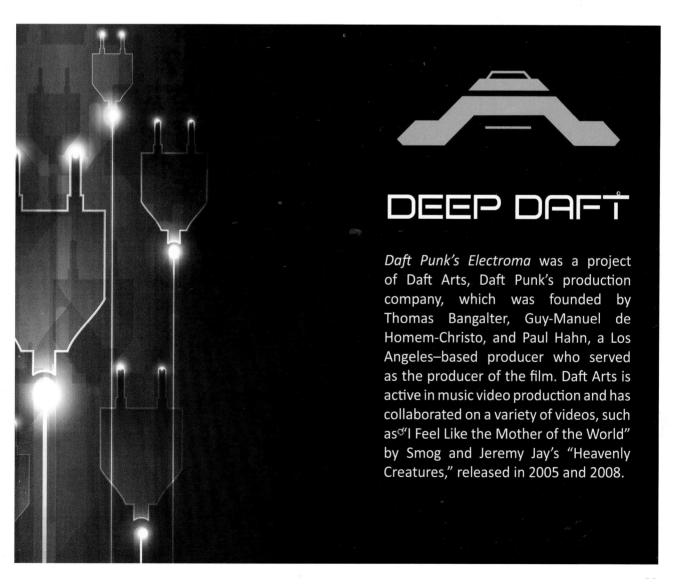

DEEP DAFT

Daft Punk's Electroma was a project of Daft Arts, Daft Punk's production company, which was founded by Thomas Bangalter, Guy-Manuel de Homem-Christo, and Paul Hahn, a Los Angeles–based producer who served as the producer of the film. Daft Arts is active in music video production and has collaborated on a variety of videos, such as "I Feel Like the Mother of the World" by Smog and Jeremy Jay's "Heavenly Creatures," released in 2005 and 2008.

his helmet—revealing a computer control panel in lieu of a face—and slams it into the ground repeatedly until it shatters. Without his significant other, he is essentially faceless and his identity is gone. Using one of the broken helmet's shards, he reflects the sunlight onto his gloved hand, setting it on fire. As the film ends, the lone robot-hero walks in slow motion through the darkness, completely ablaze.

Electroma, which premiered at the Directors' Fortnight during at the Cannes Film Festival in May 2006, was intended as a low-key, low-profile release. Unlike blockbuster films which open wide and ubiquitously, it was rolled out over time—similar to a music tour—at smaller cinemas for late-night screenings, à la *The Rocky Horror Picture Show* and other cult films (in Paris, at the time, it was shown on Saturdays at midnight). Some have viewed it as a sad film; others as hopeful. But if it's true, as Bangalter has said, that the only actor in *Electroma* is the spectator himself, who fills in the blanks left by the absence of dialogue with personal understanding, then perhaps the film endures as a cinematic question mark—a legacy that, with Daft Punk's penchant for mystery, seems fitting.

DEEP DAFT

Daft Punk's Electroma has been likened to other films, including several of the duo's favorites. *Electroma*'s extensive hiking scene is reminiscent of Gus Van Sant's 2002 film *Gerry*; its themes of rebellion and conformity were explored in George Lucas's visionary first feature-length film, *THX 1138* (1971); and its surreal pacing is something out of *2001: A Space Odyssey*, directed by Stanley Kubrick in 1968. And, of course, the helmet-wearing heroes in black leather call to mind the seminal *Phantom of the Paradise* by Brian De Palma.

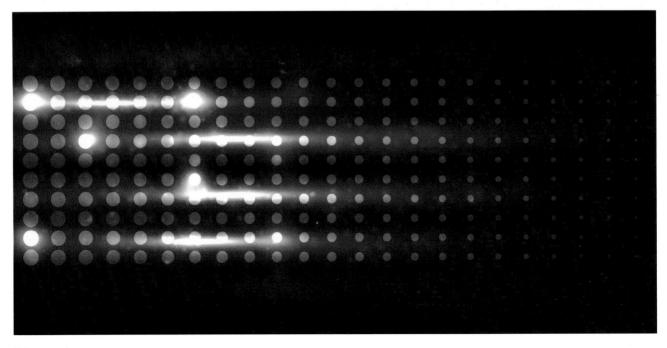

MUSIQUE, VOL. 1
1993-2005

In 2006, Daft Punk released a compilation album titled *Musique, Vol. 1 1993–2005*. *Musique*, which means "music" in French (it's also the name of the song released as the B-side to "Da Funk"), featured a CD and bonus DVD with twelve music videos, two of which were new: the Tony Gardner–helmed video for "The Prime Time of Your Life" and a black-and-white video for the remix of "Robot Rock," titled "Robot Rock (Maximum Overdrive)." The anthology, which included a bonus track in its Japanese release, reached number six on the *Billboard* Dance/Electronic Albums chart.

TRACKLIST (BONUS DVD)

"Da Funk"

"Around the World"

"Burnin'"

"Revolution 909"

"One More Time"

"Harder, Better, Faster, Stronger"

"Something About Us"

"Robot Rock"

"Technologic"

"Rollin' & Scratchin' (Live in L.A.)"

"The Prime Time of Your Life"

"Robot Rock (Maximum Overdrive)"

TRACKLIST (STANDARD CD)

"Musique"

"Da Funk"

"Around the World (Radio Edit)"

"Revolution 909"

"Alive"

"Rollin' & Scratchin'"

"One More Time (Short Radio Edit)"

"Harder, Better, Faster, Stronger"

"Something About Us"

"Robot Rock"

"Technologic (Radio Edit)"

"Human After All"

Scott Grooves's "Mothership Reconnection (Daft Punk Remix Edit)"

Ian Pooley's "Chord Memory (Daft Punk Remix)"

Gabrielle's "Forget About the World (Daft Punk 'Don't Forget the World' Mix)" (This track was replaced with "Digital Love" in the iTunes Store release; the Japanese release featured it as a sixteenth track.)

ALIVE 2006/2007

Daft Punk performs in Sydney, Australia, in December 2007.

For a genre with its roots in club culture, EDM traditionally has been more about the sound than the spectacle. DJs, the faceless ringleaders of dark, smoky hotspots, were wizards atop podiums, mixing throbbing bass lines to dancing feet and pumping fists. As EDM ventured from the dance floor to the stage, however, the transition seemed unsuited to a forum accustomed to watchers or, perhaps, wallflowers paying a ticket price rather than a cover charge.

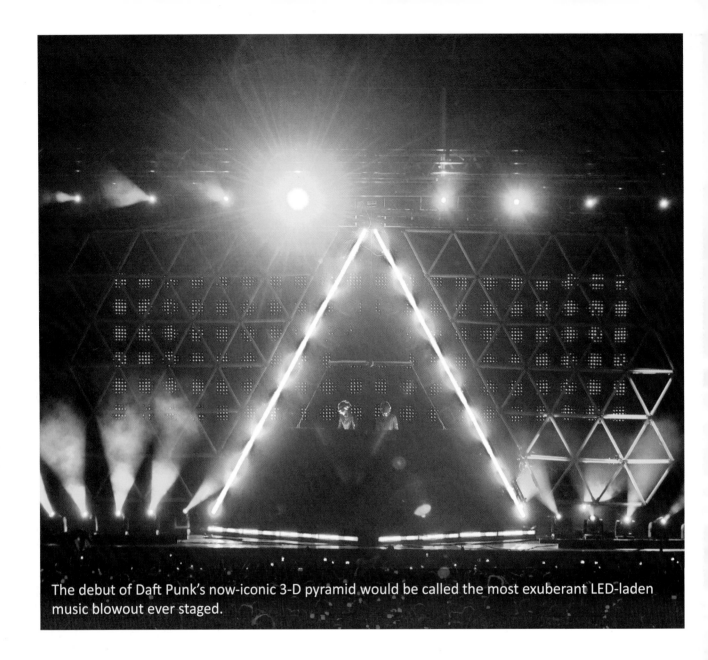

The debut of Daft Punk's now-iconic 3-D pyramid would be called the most exuberant LED-laden music blowout ever staged.

Therefore, the early days of EDM as concert attractions were off to an unsteady start with an audio/visual setup consisting of little more than a few speakers and a film projector. Although the shows changed and matured with the genre, many point to Daft Punk's first appearance at the Coachella Valley Music and Arts Festival in Indio, California, in 2006—where the duo unveiled their now-legendary pyramid—as a game-changer. Manning a 24-foot-tall aluminum pyramid of custom-built supercomputers covered with screens, Daft Punk created what many believe to be the best electronic show ever assembled, a veritable LED-infused honeycomb pulsing with music and purpose.

The idea for the pyramid stage setup came from Daft Punk's 2005 video for "Technologic," which featured a little robot who chants the song's lyrics—which flash on a television monitor—while sitting in a little red pyramid on a pyramid-themed stage where Bangalter and de Homem-Christo are playing base guitars. The two thought it would be funny to be perched in a larger pyramid in a

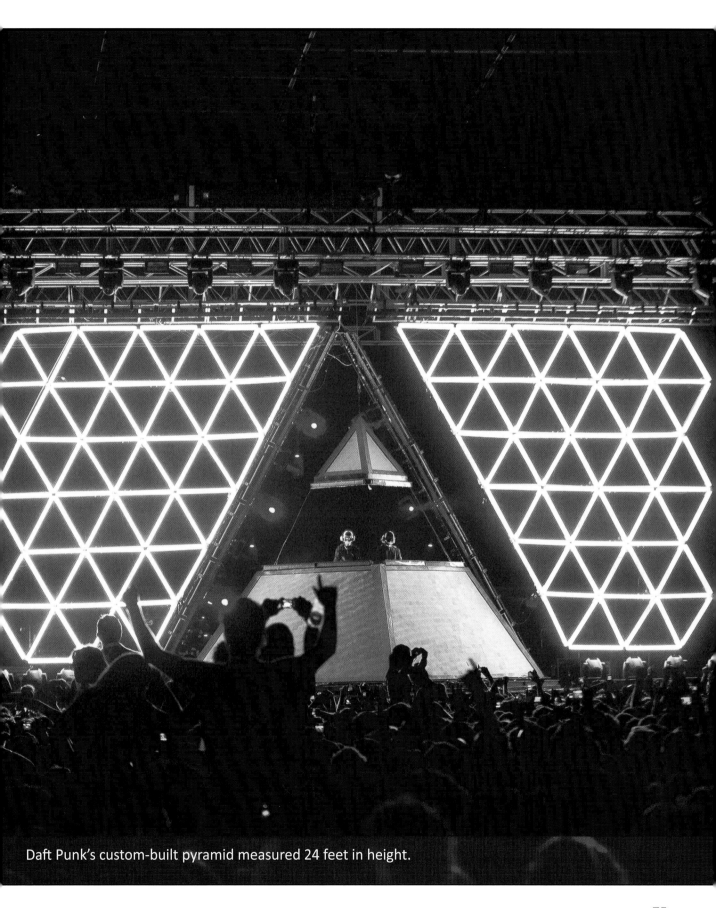

Daft Punk's custom-built pyramid measured 24 feet in height.

"crazy, tricked out show" while trying to bring a completely new and global experience to the audience.

It was with that mindset that Daft Punk began the Coachella show fittingly with the distinctive five-note sequence from the film *Close Encounters of the Third Kind*—in other words, the duo seemed to say, "Get ready to see something out of this world." What followed was just that—an hour-plus grand sound and light experience with a feast of special effects and a carefully crafted set list that nearly read like a book.

The Coachella gig—a rare live appearance in the United States—kicked off a string of festival performances that would, the following year, become a highly acclaimed and anticipated concert tour around the world advertised as "Alive 2007" (retroactively titled "Alive 2006/2007"), taking Daft Punk to Europe, South America, Asia, Mexico, and Australia as well as the United States and catapulting the French dance duo to a new tier of fame. Prior to Coachella, the duo hadn't played any shows in North America in support of its 2005 Virgin album, *Human After All*, so the men had no expectations for their return to the stage. When Daft Punk stopped playing shows in 1997 after touring for their debut album, *Homework*, the duo had been performing in front of only a couple thousand people at a clip. Nine years later, when they looked out from atop their pyramid in cities across the world, there would be tens of thousands of fans staring back.

Brooklyn, New York, August 2007.

RANDOM MEMORY

"It was an absolutely stunning performance. It had been many years since [Daft Punk] had visited the States, and that was only a very lo-fi thing in very select cities. Nobody knew what to expect when they dropped this . . . . Some YouTube commenters were struck at how little dance movement there was in the crowd, and I can say that as somebody standing twenty meters away that we were all struck dumb. After this performance, I think crowds in other cities knew what to expect, so they could just get down and rave, but for us it was a first-time experience. Standing there, you knew this was going down in history."

—Ken Moire, photographer, St. Louis, Missouri, of Daft Punk's Coachella set in 2006

ALIVE 2007

In 2007, Daft Punk released a live album, *Alive 2007*. This album featured the duo's performance at the Palais Omnisports de Paris-Bercy in Paris, a stop on the wildly successful Alive 2006/2007 global tour. Although the album's physical release was delayed until December in North America because of production issues, a digital download version became available in November of that year.

Both the album's tracklist and the tour's setlist mixed Daft Punk's popular back catalog with renewed fervor and a heavy emphasis on tracks from the third studio album *Human After All* (although *Human After All* garnered mixed reviews when first released, the live versions of the songs were well-received). *Alive 2007,* which came ten years after Daft Punk's first live album, *Alive 1997*, won the Grammy Award for Best Electronic/Dance Album in 2009. Additionally, the live version of "Harder, Better, Faster, Stronger," which was released as a single, won a Grammy Award for Best Dance Recording that year.

The album was released in CD format, and a special edition included the tour's encore on a second disk as well as a fifty-page book containing photos from the tour taken by *Random Access Memories* collaborator DJ Falcon.

DEEP DAFT

Alive 2007's single, "Harder, Better, Faster, Stronger (Alive 2007)," was released digitally in October 2007, and a music video for the track premiered online that same month. The video was inspired by the Beastie Boys' "Awesome, I Fuckin' Shot That!," a 2006 concert film that was created by giving camcorders to fifty audience members of a sold-out concert at Madison Square Garden in New York City. Similarly, the Daft Punk video featured a montage of footage shot with 250 cameras manned by audience members during a show at KeySpan Park in Brooklyn, New York. The video was directed by Olivier Gondry, a television commercial and music video director who has also worked with bands such as The Stills and Hot Hot Heat. He is the brother of Michel Gondry, who directed Daft Punk's "Around the World" video.

TRACKLIST
"Robot Rock/Oh Yeah"

"Touch It/Technologic"

"Television Rules the Nation/Crescendolls"

"Too Long/Steam Machine"

"Around the World/Harder, Better, Faster, Stronger"

"Burnin'/Too Long"

"Face to Face/Short Circuit"

"One More Time/Aerodynamic"

"Aerodynamic Beats/Forget About the World"

"The Prime Time of Your Life/The Brainwasher/Rollin' & Scratchin'/Alive"

"Da Funk/Daftendirekt"

"Superheroes/Human After All/Rock 'n Roll"

Bonus CD:
"Human After All"/"Together"/"One More Time (Reprise)"/"Music Sounds Better With You"

TRON: LEGACY

ORIGINAL MOTION PICTURE SOUNDTRACK

DISNEP

TRON
L E G A C Y

MUSIC BY DAFT PUNK

DAFT PUNK takes on film scoring with the soundtrack to *TRON: Legacy*, an album that merges their symphonic and synth-based musical interests. Having toyed with more serious material on *Human After All*, the duo continues to leave their ebullience aside and further explores their dark side with a score that features sweeping classical arrangements and crescendos coupled with pounding house tracks.

It seemed a perfect fit: Electro magnate Daft Punk, renowned for its sci-fi sound and technical innovation, providing the soundtrack for the sequel to *TRON*, the groundbreaking 1982 Walt Disney film that sought to do for cinema what the duo did for music a decade later: push the boundaries of the creative experience.

Not surprisingly, Thomas Bangalter and Guy-Manuel de Homem-Christo were fans of the original *TRON*, the story of hacker/arcade owner Kevin Flynn (played by Jeff Bridges), who is held captive in the colorful, geometric internal world of computers by an evil software known as Master Control Program (MCP). Flynn must join forces with Tron, a security program, to outmaneuver MCP and return to the real world. (De Homem-Christo has said that the original *TRON* left a "strong imprint" on him when he was eight years old.)

In 1982, with rudimentary video games just hitting the mass market (the golden age of arcade video games reached its zenith in the 1980s), there was still a naïveté surrounding computer technology, and the idea of creating an alternate universe was a source of both wonder and intrigue . . . not

TRON: LEGACY
THE PLOT

TRON: Legacy picks up twenty-plus years after the original *TRON*, which takes place in 1982. Kevin Flynn, who had become CEO of ENCOM International, disappeared in 1989, and now his son, Sam, is ENCOM's primary shareholder despite the fact that he has little interest in the business. Alan Bradley (played by Bruce Boxleitner in both films) asks Sam to investigate a strange message that seems to have come from Flynn's shuttered video arcade. There, Sam discovers a large computer in a hidden basement, and he is suddenly teleported to the Grid, the virtual reality created by his father in the original film. Sam is captured and sent to "the Games," where he is forced to participate in a fight. When he is injured, Sam is discovered to be a human "user" and is taken before the Grid's ruling program, CLU, who resembles Sam's father as a young man. Sam is then sent to compete in a difficult Light Cycle match, but is rescued by Quorra (played by Olivia Wilde), the isomorphic algorithm (ISO) and "apprentice" of Kevin Flynn.

Quorra brings Sam to his father, who is living in hiding outside CLU's territory. Flynn reveals to Sam that he has been trapped inside this world for all this time since CLU betrayed him and took control of the Grid. Turns out, CLU sent the message to Alan in order to lure Sam into the Grid, which would open the portal to the human world for a limited time—plus, CLU knew Sam would lead him right to Flynn. CLU seeks the elder Flynn's "identity disc," which is a master key to the Grid and the only way to go through the portal. With it, CLU can go through the portal and impose its system of rule on the human world. After a final confrontation, Kevin Flynn reintegrates with CLU, destroying them both, and Sam and Quorra escape together to the real world where Sam decides to retake control of ENCOM.

unlike Daft Punk's own musical philosophy. When the duo signed on for the 2010 sequel *TRON: Legacy*, it represented their first film score and offered a taste of what it was like to work with live musicians, an experience they would explore more emphatically with their next studio album, *Random Access Memories*.

Rather than go with a traditional film composer, *TRON: Legacy* director Joseph Kosinski, a successful commercial director, wanted to try something new. He was a fan of electronic music and Daft Punk, including the work that Bangalter and de Homem-Christo had done separately, such as Bangalter's soundtrack for *Irréversible* and de Homem-Christo's work with his label, Crydamoure. Kosinski believed

ROBO OP

The official music video for the track "Derezzed" features Daft Punk walking into Flynn's Arcade—the venue created by Kevin Flynn in the original *TRON*—to play an old video game named *Derezzed*. (Olivia Wilde, who plays Quorra, makes an appearance in the game.) The video was later included as a bonus feature on the DVD and Blu-ray releases of *TRON: Legacy*.

Actor Jeff Bridges at the world premiere of *TRON: Legacy* at the El Capitan Theatre in Hollywood, California

those ventures, coupled with the duo's film *Daft Punk's Electroma*, showed a level of musicianship and songwriting that proved they were, as he has said, "more than just dance music guys." When Kosinski found out through mutual friends and colleagues that Bangalter and de Homem-Christo had an interest in working on the film, they met in Los Angeles during Daft Punk's world tour to discuss a collaboration. Bangalter and de Homem-Christo liked the ideas that the studio had for the *TRON* sequel—that it would not be identical to the first film, but expand on it. Although the duo questioned whether this project was something they could do, the Alive 2006/2007 tour had given them a jolt of energy and enthusiasm to keep on doing unexpected things. The idea of partnering with Disney to contribute music to a sci-fi odyssey to be shown on IMAX screens seemed like fertile new territory to explore.

In 2008, Disney arranged to have Daft Punk meet with several successful soundtrack composers about a potential collaboration, including Hans Zimmer, Harry Gregson-Williams, John Powell, and Christophe Beck. "They were very generous and very open, sharing a lot of technical advice," Bangalter has said. However, in the end, Daft Punk scrapped any collaboration plans. "It was considered a huge risk for Disney," Kosinski has

TRACKLIST

"Overture"

"The Grid" (featuring Jeff Bridges)

"The Son of Flynn"

"Recognizer"

"Armory"

"Arena"

"Rinzler"

"The Game Has Changed"

"Outlands"

"Adagio for Tron"

"Nocturne"

"End of Line"

"Derezzed"

"Fall"

"Solar Sailer"

"Rectifier"

"Disc Wars"

"C.L.U."

"Arrival"

"Flynn Lives"

"Tron Legacy (End Titles)"

"Finale"

RANDOM MEMORY

"It seems complicated at the end of the day, but it's actually quite simple. I was locked in a room with robots for almost two years and it was simply a lot of hard work. We were just together working throughout the whole process and there was never a point where the orchestra was not in their minds and the electronics were not in my mind. It was a continual translation between the two worlds and hopefully we put something together that will be something different because of that."

—Joseph Trapanese, music arranger, *TRON: Legacy*, during the *TRON: Legacy* Music Event

said. "A director who had never done a feature before and composers who hadn't scored a movie before."

Although the filmmakers were expecting the duo to come up with a purely electronic score, Daft Punk wanted the film to be timeless—"a cello was there 400 years ago and will still be here in 400 years," Bangalter has said, "but synthesizers that were invented twenty years ago will probably be gone in the next twenty." In their electronic music, Daft Punk has always tried to combine existing genres, so they liked the idea of merging a dark, 70s-style electronic score with a classic Hollywood sound for the *TRON: Legacy* musical score.

Scoring began in earnest in January 2009, even though there was still no script, only concept drawings. Bangalter and de Homem-Christo decided to limit themselves to six or seven digital sounds, which they would embed—like virtual instruments—within an orchestra. (Bangalter has said he composed the soundtrack's heroic themes, while de Homem-Christo wrote the darker musical cues.) In July 2010, Daft Punk assembled a symphony of eighty-five world-class musicians in London and recorded the orchestra at AIR Lyndhurst Studios, Britain's premier scoring facility. They worked with music arranger and orchestrator Joseph Trapanese, who translated the duo's ideas into symphonic arrangements—"my role was as the interface between the robots and the orchestra," Trapanese has joked. The result was a dark and ominous score that would rely as much on classical orchestrations as on electronics, merging poignant strings and horns with pulsing bass and synth. "We knew from the start that there was no way we were going to do this film score with two synthesizers and a drum machine," Bangalter has said.

PRETTY IN PUNK

Disney Consumer Products collaborated with consumer electronics company Monster Cable and specialty toy maker Medicom Toy for Daft Punk–inspired *TRON: Legacy* electronics and toys:

▸ Monster's specially lighted Daft Punk Edition *TRON* headphones were specifically designed for gaming, music, and home cinema, and were released with a special surround-sound mix of the *TRON: Legacy* original motion picture soundtrack.

▸ Known for its signature Kubrick and Bearbrick figures, Medicom Toy released the Series 21 Bearbrick assortment, 400% Bearbrick two-pack, Kubrick two-pack, and 12-inch Real Action Heroes figures designed to match the *TRON: Legacy* suits worn by Daft Punk in their film cameo.

ROBO OP

Daft Punk makes a cameo in *TRON: Legacy,* appearing as DJ programs at the Castor's End of the Line Club. Although the duo's robot masks were a natural for the world of *TRON*, Thomas Bangalter and Guy-Manuel de Homem-Christo received new helmets and suits that were in line with the vibe of the scene. Bangalter has said the film cameo was "as fun as being in *Star Wars,*" referring to the 2010 Adidas commercial in which the robots appear in a star-studded version of the famous "Cantina scene."

TRON: LEGACY: THE CAST & CREW

- Kevin Flynn/CLU: Jeff Bridges comes from a well-known acting family that includes Lloyd Bridges and his brother, Beau. Bridges began his acting career in 1958 with his father and brother on the television series *Sea Hunt*. He has been in many films, including *The Last Picture Show, Starman, The Fabulous Baker Boys, Jagged Edge, Against All Odds, Seabiscuit*, and cult favorite *The Big Lebowski*. He won the Academy Award for Best Actor for his role as Otis "Bad" Blake in the 2009 film *Crazy Heart*.

- Sam Flynn: Garrett Hedlund is known for his roles in the films *Friday Night Lights, Four Brothers, Eragon, Country Strong*, and *On the Road*.

- Quorra: Olivia Wilde has appeared in a number of television and film productions, including *The O.C., The Black Donnellys,* and *Cowboys & Aliens*. She is best known for playing "13" on the long-running series *House*.

- Alan Bradley/Tron: Bruce Boxleitner is an actor and science fiction/suspense writer. He has starred in several television series: *How the West Was Won, Bring 'Em Back Alive, Scarecrow and Mrs. King*, and *Babylon 5*. He also provided the voice of "Tron" for the animated series, *TRON: Uprising*.

- Director: Best known for his computer graphics and imagery work, Joseph Kosinski made his big-screen directorial debut with *TRON: Legacy*. His previous work included CGI-related television commercials, including *Halo 3*'s "Starry Night" and the award-winning "Mad World" for *Gears of War*.

- Music arranger/orchestrator: Joseph Trapanese has worked in the production of music for films, television, theater, and concerts. Original composition projects include the film *Oblivion*, the animated series *TRON: Uprising*, and the Web series *The Bannen Way*. He also contributed arrangements to *Percy Jackson & the Olympians: The Lightning Thief, What Happens in Vegas,* and *Traitor,* as well as orchestrations for several seasons of the cable series *Dexter*.

Andy Warhol was an early Daft Punk influence.

Daft Punk's artistic vision uses music to develop various vectors of artistic expression, satellites that piece together into a comprehensive whole. From Thomas Bangalter and Guy-Manuel de Homem-Christo's cutting-edge and elaborate set design to their costuming, choreographed live shows, and highly selective media appearances, there is an air of theatricality and performance to all that they do that transcends the music business as an ever-evolving vision of art.

Part of that vision includes outright commercialization, an area that some artists tend to—or, at least, *pretend* to—shy away from. For a couple of guys who like to keep their distance from the press, Bangalter and de Homem-Christo make a point of showing up in the mass media from time to time, whether in corporate commercials or video games, in order to maintain that interactive engagement with their audience. Much like Andy Warhol (the leading figure in the visual art movement known as Pop Art and an early influence of the duo) Daft Punk has deftly straddled the realms of art and pop culture—that delicate balance between art as a craft and also as an industry—since the beginning of their career, exploring the relationship between artistic expression, celebrity, and advertisement. In doing so, they have become pop culture icons.

1996

▸ *Wipeout 2097*, a racing video game, features the Daft Punk song "Musique" on its in-game soundtrack. This is one of the duo's earliest commercial tie-ins.

2001

▸ Daft Punk trades in their black leather for relaxed denim in a commercial for The Gap that has them dancing (and doing the robot) to their song "Digital Love" with actress Juliette Lewis (she was nominated for an Academy Award for her supporting role in the 1991 film *Cape Fear*), who is gussied up in flared denim and a jaunty hat.

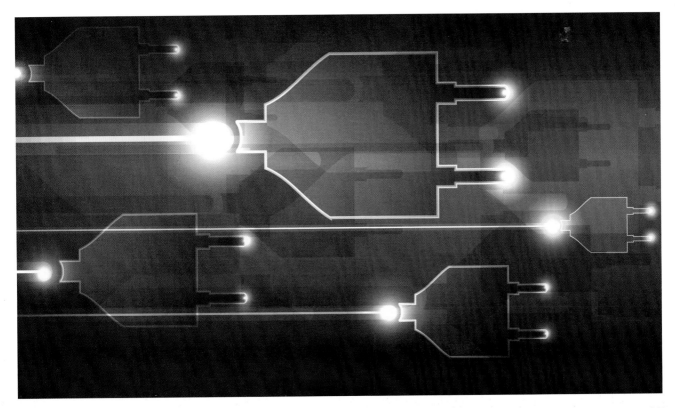

2005

▸ When Apple launches its silhouette campaign for the iPod, the company features Daft Punk's "Technologic" prominently in one commercial. The song is also featured in an ad for the Motorola E398 mobile phone, which airs in Brazil.

▸ The Daft Punk single "Technologic" is featured on Episode 19 of *The O.C.* in a rager scene that takes place at Caleb's mansion.

2006

▸ The robots are tapped to launch Sony Ericsson's Premini mobile phone in a Japanese ad.

2007

▸ French fashion house Louis Vuitton asks Daft Punk to create a mix for its Spring/Summer 2008 fashion show.

▸ Thomas Bangalter appears as his robot self in a DVD from Chilly Gonzales (credited as Gonzales) titled *From Major to Minor,* and performs various musical exercises in front of a live audience.

▸ In the *Flight of the Conchords* episode "Sally," a music video for the Flight of the Conchords' song "Robots" is shot with homemade robot costumes fashioned by the band's manager, Murray. Jemaine comments, "It doesn't look like Daft Punk. We wanted ones like Daft Punk."

2009

▸ Daft Punk lends its image and eleven mixes [there's a mix of Queen's "We Will Rock You" and Daft Punk's "Robot Rock" called "We Will (Robot) Rock You"] to the video game *DJ Hero*, a rhythm game that's a spin-off of the popular *Guitar Hero* franchise. The duo, who have their own venue in the game, also appear as a pair of playable characters wearing their *Discovery*-era helmets and *Human After All*–era leather duds.

(For the launch of the video game, Daft Punk stars in a fully animated commercial showing the duo on stage.) Although Daft Punk's playable likenesses were absent from the sequel, *DJ Hero 2*, the game includes a remixed version of the song "Human After All."

▸ "Technologic" is used in a Lincoln MKS commercial and in a series of TV ads for the Alfa Romeo MiTo.

Jermaine Clement and Bret McKenzie of Flight of the Conchords performing in Vancouver, British Columbia.

2010

- ▶ "Robot Rock" plays during a fight scene in the film *Iron Man 2*, which stars Robert Downey Jr. The film was a critical and commercial success, grossing $623.9 million at the worldwide box office.

- ▶ Britain's Myleene Klass plays Daft Punk's "Aerodynamic" during a Pantene Pro-V commercial.

- ▶ As part of its launch of a series of *Star Wars*–branded shoes and clothing, Adidas unveils an advertisement that's a star-studded reenactment of the famous Mos Eisley Cantina scene from George Lucas's *Star Wars Episode IV*. The scene reimagines original footage from the film with new cast members including Snoop Lion (then Snoop Dogg), Ciara, David Beckham, Ian Brown, Oasis, Jay Baruchel, and Daft Punk, who gather alongside Han Solo, Chewbacca, C-3PO, and Obi-Wan Kenobi.

2011

- ▶ Daft Punk designs limited edition Coca-Cola bottles (known as "Daft Coke") that feature its logo on the caps (colored silver or gold to match their helmets). The bottles, which are available exclusively in France, later become collector's items; bottles sell on eBay for hundreds of dollars.

2012

▸ Daft Punk makes a cameo (sort of) on *The Simpsons* when Discotheque Stuart (also known as Disco Stu, owner of Stu's Disco) strides past Homer and Marge on the street wearing a Bangalter-esque robot mask.

2013

▸ Hedi Slimane photographs Daft Punk for the Saint Laurent Music Project, a portrait series that draws on the relationship between music icons and the fashion house. In the black-and-white visuals shot in Los Angeles, the duo are dressed in stagewear by Slimane for Saint Laurent, including a black glitter jacket, "Le Smoking."

▸ Additionally, Daft Punk was the first choice to create the soundtrack for Slimane's first show as creative director for the recently rebranded label in October 2012.

▸ After Game 1 of the Stanley Cup Finals, Deadspin.com uses "Technologic" as the beat for a compilation of passing and shooting calls (all 140 of them) from sports announcer Mike "Doc" Emrick.

▸ Daft Punk's chart-topping "Get Lucky" is added to the *Just Dance 2014* tracklist. The duo joins recording artists such as Robin Thicke, Nicki Minaj, One Direction, Psy, Robbie Williams, Ke$ha, and Rihanna, who also have tracks featured on the popular dance video game.

Miley Cyrus and Robin Thicke paired up at the *2013 MTV Video Music Awards* to sing "Blurred Lines," the chart-topping song that joins Daft Punk's "Get Lucky" on the *Just Dance 2014* tracklist.

THE HELMETS AND OUTFITS

Not many world-renowned celebrities can ride the subways unrecognized or walk undetected among the crowds at their own concert. What began as a reaction to being shy has turned into a fixture of Daft Punk's brand: the helmet. Creating an advanced version of glam that draws a solid line between fiction and reality (similar to the personas created by Kraftwerk, David Bowie's Ziggy Stardust, and KISS), Thomas Bangalter and Guy-Manuel de Homem-Christo found that by trying to circumvent the media, they developed an exciting aspect of their art. "We've just been trying to do cool stuff and interesting stuff in every creative domain, with every art form we could use," Bangalter has said.

While most artists accept—albeit begrudgingly—television and other media appearances as part of their promotional duties, early on Bangalter and de Homem-Christo questioned that philosophy, proposing that perhaps artists can act and live differently and still make a lasting public impression, all while having a private everyday life—what Bangalter once called "a Wizard of Oz situation."

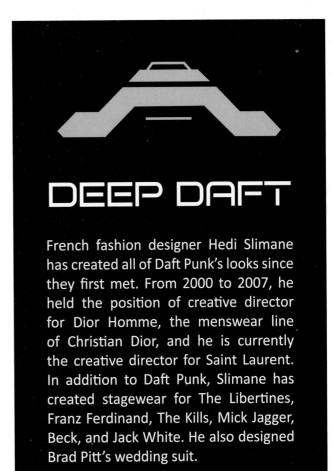

DEEP DAFT

French fashion designer Hedi Slimane has created all of Daft Punk's looks since they first met. From 2000 to 2007, he held the position of creative director for Dior Homme, the menswear line of Christian Dior, and he is currently the creative director for Saint Laurent. In addition to Daft Punk, Slimane has created stagewear for The Libertines, Franz Ferdinand, The Kills, Mick Jagger, Beck, and Jack White. He also designed Brad Pitt's wedding suit.

Like David Bowie's Ziggy Stardust, Daft Punk's robot persona draws upon a fictionalized glam.

THE *HOMEWORK* YEARS (PRE-HELMET ERA)

In the mid 90s, Bangalter and de Homem-Christo wear masks to hide their appearance and are not averse to placing black bags on their heads during promotional appearances or wearing simple (yet creepy) Halloween masks at photo shoots.

ROBO OP

A YouTube video titled "How to make a Daft Punk helmet in 17 months" has more than three million views.

THE *DISCOVERY* YEARS

This era, which lasts from the late 90s to the early 00s, marks the official launch of the robot persona and the complex robot helmet. The (now defunct) LED specialist company LED FX is credited with creating the helmets, although it is thought that Tony Gardner and special effects company Alterian engineered them. The helmets feature intricate LED displays that can display text and sync images and patterns to music, and there is a ribbed neck covering. (Wigs were originally attached to both helmets, but the duo decided to remove them before the outfits were publicly unveiled in 2001.) Photographs of the duo in their helmets appear in French magazines a month before *Discovery* drops: de Homem-Christo's was gold and featured a rainbow-flanked smiley face in lights; Bangalter's was silver with a narrow red visor. Tiny wires cascaded from the back of the helmets to control boards in their backpacks.

Early in their career, Thomas Bangalter and Guy-Manuel de Homem-Christo sometimes wore masks rather than helmets to disguise their faces in photos.

The duo's *Discovery* helmets featured colorful and intricate LED displays.

THE *HUMAN AFTER ALL* YEARS

From 2005 to 2010, Daft Punk's outfits become slightly less complicated, consisting of dark leather jumpsuits designed by Hedi Slimane and simplified, LED-less headgear. Both visors are now black. (Between *Discovery* and *Human After All*, Daft Punk wore what are considered "transition helmets" that were similar to the *Human After All* helmets in size, shape, and detail.) One notable change regarding Bangalter's helmet from *Discovery* to *Human After All* is the removal of the "smile," which is replaced by just a slit. Also, new gloves, which appear to be elbow-length, are made out of a Lycra/Spandex material, with pads in the fingertips to make it easier to play instruments. Neither wears the ribbed neck covering any longer.

PRETTY IN PUNK

Daft Punk's *Human After All* helmets served as the basis for their "encore" helmets, which were created by Janet Hansen of Enlighted Designs and used during the encore of Daft Punk's Alive 2007 tour. Enlighted installed several hundred feet of red EL wire on each leather jacket, following the seam lines and styling details. The Daft Punk logo on the back of each jacket (originally written with metal studs) was recreated with some three hundred red LEDs. For the lighted helmets, the company attached EL wire to matte black replicas of the duo's metallic helmets that were worn for the earlier part of the show.

Daft Punk wore these red-lined helmets during the encore for their Alive 2006/2007 concert tour.

THE *TRON: LEGACY* YEARS

Daft Punk's helmet production is taken over by Ironhead Studios, the special effects company working on the film. The helmets feature a dull metal sheen and white/light blue LEDs.

THE *RANDOM ACCESS MEMORIES* YEARS

While the helmets retain their respective silver and gold signatures, the robots go glam, appearing as glittery androids and sporting sequins.

RANDOM MEMORY

"I remember when I was a kid, I would watch *Superman,* and I was super into the feeling of knowing that Clark Kent is Superman and no one knows. We always thought as we were shaping this thing that the fantasy was actually so much more exciting than the idea of being the most famous person in the world."

—Thomas Bangalter to *GQ* magazine in May 2013

Daft Punk goes sci-fi glam for *Random Access Memories.*

RANDOM ACCESS MEMORIES: THE BUILDUP

FILLED WITH live, in-studio collaborations, Daft Punk's long-awaited fourth studio album, *Random Access Memories*, offers an impressive collection of talent, laced with choirs, orchestras, and big-name guest musicians. Over-the-top campy one minute, smooth and silky the next, the album arrives in a blaze of glory that's preceded by an ironically quiet, albeit tantalizing, rollout.

By 2011, after the excitement surrounding Daft Punk's involvement with *TRON: Legacy* settled, talk turned to new material; the duo hadn't released a studio album since 2005's *Human After All*. Music journalists, bloggers, and fans began scrounging for whatever crumbs of information they could find online (a mention by Chic's renowned Nile Rodgers here, another by the eccentric pianist Chilly Gonzales there) until, bit by bit, they pieced together that . . . well, only that Daft Punk was up to *something* collaborative. What it was and when it would be released was anyone's guess.

By 2013, Daft Punk was ready to spill, but rather than doing the music industry's typical full-throttle promotional blitz, the duo focused on an old-school rollout or "seduction," as Thomas Bangalter has called it—"a process of tempting, of teasing, of creating desire." The result was a viral cat-and-mouse game that not only had the media and music fans in a virtual frenzy, but that also gave them a chance to fill in the blanks on their own and become part of the publicity process thanks to the scarcity of comprehensive and concrete information.

Random Access Memories billboard, Stockholm, Sweden, 2013.

January 2013

▸ January 4: Having already divulged news of an upcoming partnership with the French duo back in 2012, Chic's Rodgers writes on his blog that by the next time he visits Japan his collaboration with Daft Punk will have "started to hit people's eardrums," which gives eagerly awaiting fans their first timetable for the new project: 2013.

▸ January 26: The French newspaper *Le Parisien* reports that Daft Punk has left EMI's Virgin Records—the label they signed with back in 1996—and moved to Sony's Columbia Records for their forthcoming album. The information apparently comes from a conversation Guy-Manuel de Homem-Christo had with friends while at an album launch party for Kavinsky, a French house artist. That same day, *The Hollywood Reporter* notes that Daft Punk turned down a "gigantic sum of money" to perform at 2013's Coachella festival. Still, the news does not stop speculation that the French duo will show up for an unannounced cameo appearance, considering long-time pals Phoenix are one of the festival's headliners.

▸ January 28: *The Guardian* reports that Daft Punk's new album, whose title has not yet been revealed, will drop in May.

February 2013

▸ February 26: Daft Punk confirms its alliance with Columbia Records when an image is added to the duo's Facebook page displaying the halves of two helmets—one silver and one gold—alongside the Columbia logo. (The new album is to be released by the duo's imprint Daft Life, under exclusive license to Columbia Records.) The same image appears on Daft Punk's Web site; the stunt attracts millions to the site on the first day.

March 2013

▸ March 2: The first of three short commercials makes its debut during *Saturday Night Live*—a fifteen-second teaser ad featuring a blinged-out Daft Punk logo with an instrumental snippet of the album's first single, "Get Lucky."

▸ Early March: Billboards and posters (similar in design to the French duo's uploaded artwork on Facebook) begin popping up in cities across the globe, including Los Angeles, London, New York, and Paris. Bangalter and de Homem-Christo, fond of the 2012 book *Rock 'n' Roll Billboards of the Sunset Strip* by photographer Robert Landau,

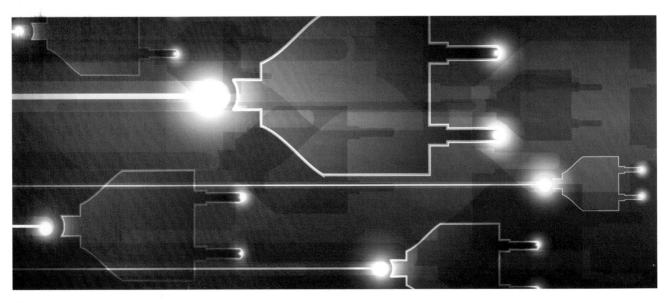

Daft Punk billboard and wind turbines on the way to Coachella, April 19, 2013.

strive to replicate how album releases were promoted on billboards in LA during the 60s and 70s. "They became iconic symbols of that landscape," Bangalter has said. Photos of the Daft Punk billboards and posters go viral, with one fan creating a Reddit page that maps all the international Daft Punk billboard sightings, and The Daft Club, a Daft Punk fan site, aggregating fans' uploaded billboard images.

▸ March 18: Sony registers thirteen untitled tracks (ranging in length from 3:48 to 9:04) via Phonographic Performance Limited (PPL), the UK-based group that licenses recorded music and distributes royalties. This gives fans their first, albeit vague, glimpse of what to expect on the new album.

▸ March 23: Daft Punk drops a second *SNL* ad that reveals the new album's title: *Random Access Memories*. Like its predecessor, this spot only airs once and includes the music from "Get Lucky," without ever mentioning the song title or the album's release date. The ad placement sparks lots of Twitter buzz, with forty-one times more tweets posted about the Daft Punk spot than any other aired during the show—and, in fact, more tweets than about the *SNL* episode itself.

April 2013

▸ April 3: In collaboration with The Creators Project (a global partnership between Intel and Vice that's dedicated to the celebration of art and technology), Daft Punk launches a series of short documentaries that detail the backgrounds of the *Random Access Memories* collaborators. Episode One features legendary disco innovator Giorgio Moroder.

▸ April 9: It is announced that on May 17 the small town of Wee Waa (population: 2,000) in New South Wales, Australia, will host the global album launch for Daft Punk's fourth studio album. *Random Access Memories* will be unveiled at the 79th annual Wee Waa Show, an agricultural festival renowned for featuring some of New South Wales's finest sheep and cattle, and played in full to 4,000 ticket holders. The event sells out in thirteen minutes.

▸ April 12: Although Daft Punk does not perform at Coachella as rumored, the French duo manage to amp up the crowd on the festival's first day by broadcasting a trailer for their upcoming new album on the main stage Jumbotrons right before the Yeah Yeah Yeahs take the stage for their set. The video, which runs under two minutes, features Daft Punk playing guitar and drums alongside vocalist Pharrell Williams and Chic's Rodgers on guitar for the track "Get Lucky." The video also confirms a list of guests to appear on the album, which, in addition to Williams and Rodgers, is set to feature Moroder, Animal Collective's Panda Bear, The Strokes frontman Julian Casablancas, house music producer Todd Edwards, DJ Falcon, Chilly Gonzales, and 70s singer/songwriter Paul Williams. (Little do Coachella goers know that Bangalter and de Homem-Christo are standing right there among them, helmet-less, watching the Jumbotron screens from the festival's VIP section.)

▸ April 13: The third *SNL* spot airs—a one-minute video similar to what appeared at Coachella the day before (sans collaborator list)—with pre-order information (*Random Access Memories* pre-orders reached the #2 slot on iTunes). That same day, *Rolling Stone* publishes the first in a slew of media interviews granted by Daft Punk to discuss *Random Access Memories*—a far cry from the duo's close-lipped approach for their last studio album, *Human After All.* Bangalter has said that since *RAM* was more than five years in the making, including three years—"happy times"—of working collaboratively with singers, musicians, sound engineers, and technicians, it seemed "logical and responsible to promote generosity" in terms of the album's publicity efforts.

▸ April 16: Daft Punk releases the tracklist for its new album via a Twitter video app called Vine, which is posted to the Columbia Records account.

▸ April 17: Although the song "Get Lucky" is purported to have been leaked numerous times already (many of the fakes consisting of a series

Eugene Cernan, commander of Apollo 17, appears in a video series chronicling the stories behind the songs of *Random Access Memories*.

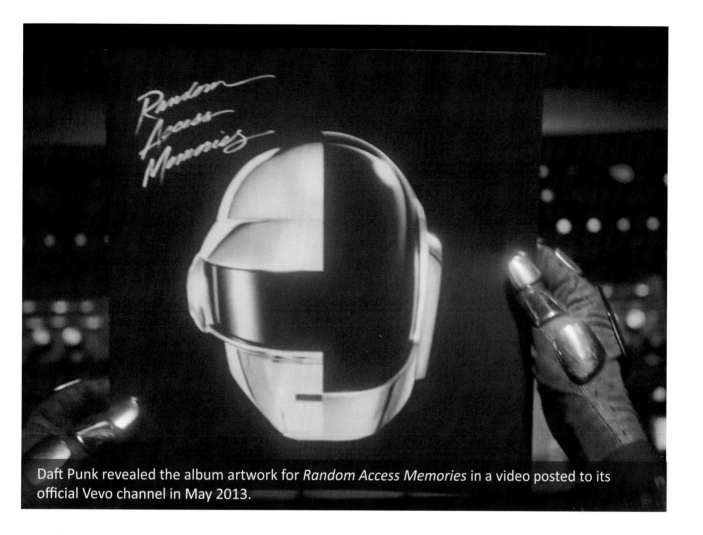

Daft Punk revealed the album artwork for *Random Access Memories* in a video posted to its official Vevo channel in May 2013.

of stitched together "Get Lucky" loops from the ads), the real deal hits the virtual airwaves when a radio edit of the song goes viral.

▶ April 19: Columbia makes "Get Lucky" available for download at 12:01 A.M. The Internet explodes with various covers of the song in the weeks that follow and throughout the rest of the summer, including a rendition performed by Orthodox Jews for Rosh Hashanah the following September.

May 2013

▶ May 13: Daft Punk's official Vevo channel posts a space-age video that features the Daft Punk robots revealing the artwork and packaging of the vinyl version of *Random Access Memories*,

as well as the first few seconds of the opening track. Later that day, a limited-time preview stream of the full album is launched via the iTunes Store.

▶ May 17: The day of what was to have been the world premiere of *Random Access Memories* in Wee Waa seems a bit anticlimactic since the album has already been made available online. Although the show still goes on, attendance is reportedly down (it is said that the local Wee Waa Motel experienced many cancellations the day following the leak).

▶ May 21: Columbia releases *Random Access Memories*, which makes its debut at #1 on the *Billboard* 200 chart.

THE NEW SOUND

After an eight-year hiatus, the robots are back. And they've got company.

One of the most highly anticipated records of the decade, *Random Access Memories (RAM)*, the fourth studio album from Daft Punk, is both a return and a departure for the French music duo, melding dance, rock, funk, kitsch, and even Broadway-style pop presented in—*surprise!*—the fat, saturated sound of analog tape and processing. This time around, the robots ditched their sampling—a technique they practically pioneered in EDM—because it struck them as increasingly canned and cliché, and opted instead to have *humans* join them for live sessions in the recording studio. In other words, Daft Punk has moved forward by starting again.

Inspired by classic albums from boundary-pushing artists such as The Eagles's *Hotel California*, Fleetwood Mac's *Rumors*, and Pink Floyd's *Dark Side of the Moon*, *Random Access Memories* hearkens back to a time before compact discs and Walkmans allowed music fans to skip over songs. The album, estimated as costing more than 1 million dollars to produce and promote, is a gold-plated homage to the 70s and 80s—a period that de Homem-Christo has called "the tastiest era" for Daft Punk—and a reminder that creativity can sometimes be found anywhere but here. Daft Punk seems to say that the current trend of surrendering oneself entirely to the technology of music doesn't really compute. Although "random access memory" (or RAM) is certainly helpful as a form of computer data storage, memories (with an S) are produced only by the mind, and the two—man and machine—need to work together. Similarly, EDM, beset with turnkey systems, including preset banks and sounds, has grown increasingly homogenized—new songs resemble what's already out there, creating a vicious cycle of sameness—and could use a bit of a reboot. To do that, Daft Punk has taken the computers out of the studio (they attempted to express themselves using a laptop, but were unsuccessful) and brought history and the team mentality that is at the core of other industries, such as film production, back to music making. This move is announced, literally, by the title of the first track: "Give Life Back to Music."

Chilly Gonzales

Songs on this album span years and geography. Daft Punk recorded the album in legendary studios in New York, Paris, and Los Angeles with musicians including groundbreaking producer Giorgio Moroder, Chic mastermind Nile Rodgers, The Neptunes's Pharrell Williams, pianist and producer Chilly Gonzales, Julian Casablancas of The Strokes, Animal Collective's Panda Bear, and session players, including John "JR" Robinson, from Michael Jackson's *Off the Wall and Thriller.* (Interestingly, much has been made of the *Random Access Memories* album cover's likeness to that of the cover for Michael Jackson's landmark 1982 album *Thriller*). Schmaltz king Paul Williams (who composed the opening theme to *The Love Boat*) wrote the lyrics for two songs on the album,

"Beyond" and "Touch," a complex and quirky mini-opera on which he also sings. Rodgers provides his smooth, recognizable guitar riffs from the get-go, as well as on the tracks "Lose Yourself to Dance" and "Get Lucky," where he's joined by Pharrell Williams on lead vocals. "Get Lucky," a song one reviewer said could be listened to billions of times without tiring, would be nominated for "Best Song of the Summer" at the 2013 MTV Video Music Awards, reaching the Top 10 in more than thirty-two countries, and becoming certified Gold or Platinum in more than ten nations within a few months of its release. It also had the biggest streaming day for a single track in the history of Spotify for the United States and United Kingdom, as well as the biggest first day in the music streaming service's history.

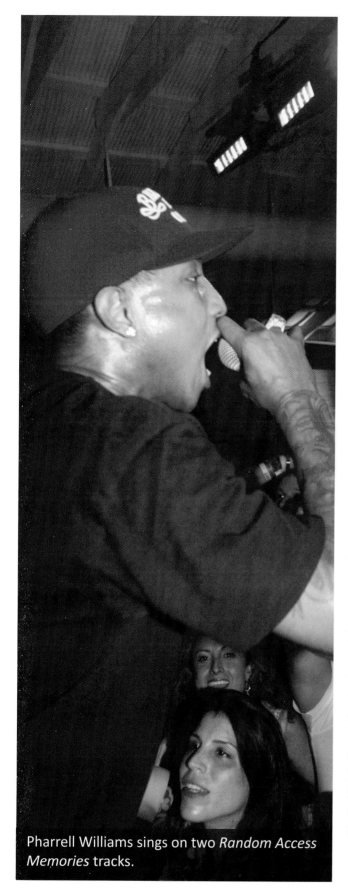

Pharrell Williams sings on two *Random Access Memories* tracks.

The mega-success of *Random Access Memories'* "Get Lucky," with its breezy, effectively simple hook, highlights an ambitious assembly of people, instruments, and ideas—from the progressive to the peculiar. Joining the robots' vocoder-filtered voices and synthpop ways are a choir, an orchestra, pedal-steel players, trumpeters, and some sound effects straight from a Foley-stage, forming a cohesive, sometimes puzzling, but altogether entertaining seventy-four minutes.

"The Game of Love," a downtempo jazzy number features Robinson on drums and the sorrowful singing of a broken-hearted robot (neither Bangalter nor de Homem-Christo ever divulge which of the two is at the microphone). It's followed by "Giorgio by Moroder," a striking bit of pop-prog in which Moroder, who has been kind of a mythical figure for Daft Punk, provides a spoken, docu-style monologue about his life as a musician. "Within," a minimalist piece that features Gonzales on piano, contrasts with the textured, futuristic instrumental "Motherboard," which is full of fluttery woodwinds and all kinds of synths. Casablancas adds his velvety vocals to the melodic "Instant Crush," while legendary house producer Todd Edwards—with whom Daft Punk worked on the *Discovery* album—sings on "Fragments of Time," its squealing lap-slide guitar riffs calling to mind the days of Hall & Oates.

As the album plays to its conclusion, Panda Bear's angelic entreaties on the uplifting "Doin' It Right" lead into "Contact," the last track, which features the album's only samples, pulling its main riff from the song "We Ride Tonight" by The Sherbs, as well as the voice of Captain Eugene Cernan of Apollo 17, the last man to leave the surface of the moon on the final Apollo mission. The song feels like a fitting summation, if only to serve as a reminder that however far away the final frontier may be, whether in space or in song, it's always nice to be able to come back home.

RANDOM ACCESS MEMORIES: THE STUDIOS

Some say that Capitol Studios' round shape echoes that of a stack of records.

Random Access Memories was the first studio album to take Daft Punk out of the bedroom and into a proper studio—and with good reason. The whole starting point of the album, Thomas Bangalter has said, was "to somehow question the magical powers of recorded audio" at a time when popular music seemed to be relying more heavily on computers and sampling.

Since the beginning, samples had been a tenet of both Daft Punk's music production and the development of electronic dance music as a genre. For perhaps the first time, the duo began to wonder why. Bangalter and Guy-Manuel de Homem-Christo took a look at the classic music of the past and decided to deconstruct the parameters of its craftsmanship—the performances, the hardware engineers, and the studios—to see if they could recreate records at that level of production. To do that, they not only decided to partner with musicians from that golden age, but also to record in five venerable studios where, for many years, music magic had been made.

CAPITOL STUDIOS,
HOLLYWOOD

Since its completion in 1956, Capitol Studios has been a staple of the recording industry. The studios are located in the Capitol Records Building (also known as the Capitol Records Tower), an iconic structure in the heart of Hollywood that's modern, striking, and earthquake-resistant. The ground floor (which is the only rectangular part of the building) houses the recording department offices, two mastering rooms, three recording studios, and six production/editing rooms. (Because they are subterranean concrete bunkers built thirty feet underground, the Capitol Studios are said to feature unique echo chambers.) Iconic artists such as Nat King Cole and The Beach Boys first gave life to its rooms, which continue to be used by an array of popular musicians more than fifty years later.

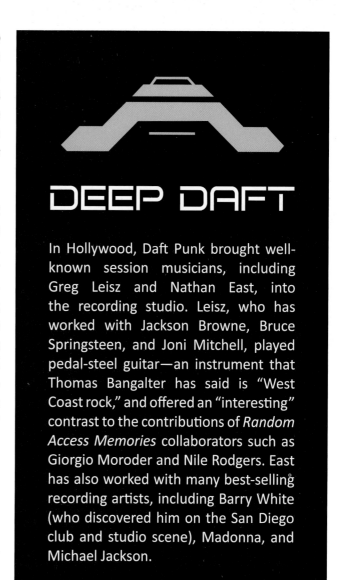

DEEP DAFT

In Hollywood, Daft Punk brought well-known session musicians, including Greg Leisz and Nathan East, into the recording studio. Leisz, who has worked with Jackson Browne, Bruce Springsteen, and Joni Mitchell, played pedal-steel guitar—an instrument that Thomas Bangalter has said is "West Coast rock," and offered an "interesting" contrast to the contributions of *Random Access Memories* collaborators such as Giorgio Moroder and Nile Rodgers. East has also worked with many best-selling recording artists, including Barry White (who discovered him on the San Diego club and studio scene), Madonna, and Michael Jackson.

HENSON RECORDING
STUDIOS, HOLLYWOOD

In 1917, Charlie Chaplin founded a motion picture studio, Chaplin Studios, on La Brea Avenue in Hollywood. After several changes of ownership, the property was bought by Herb Alpert and Jerry Moss and their record company, A&M Records, in 1966; they transformed one of the lot's two soundstages into a recording studio. The studio opened in 1968 (Sergio Mendes & Brasil '66's

The Fool on the Hill was the first album to credit A&M Records) and was designated a Los Angeles Historic-Culture Monument in 1969, the same year mixing/cutting rooms and reverberation chambers were added. (Bangalter has said the concrete on the floor and walls still shows because while the studio was being constructed in the 70s, the "engineers loved the sound so much as it was that they decided not to finish.") In 1999, A&M was sold to Universal Music, and the studio was purchased by The Jim Henson Company.

Over the years, the studio has hosted an array of musical clients that includes Phil Spector (60s); The Supremes, John Lennon, and The Doors (70s); KISS, Bon Jovi, and Supertramp (80s); Melissa Etheridge, The Rolling Stones, and Dr. Dre (90s); and Ozzy Osbourne, Pearl Jam, and Ziggy Marley (00s). As *Random Access Memories* collaborator Todd Edwards has said of recording there with Daft Punk, "It is really vibe-y and you just feel a presence."

CONWAY RECORDING STUDIOS, HOLLYWOOD

Located in the historic Paramount Pictures district, Conway Recording Studios was an eight-track studio purchased by Buddy and Susan Brundo in 1976 and turned into a prestigious world-class recording facility. Designed with a resort-like aesthetic (its three studios are surrounded by lush tropical and desert gardens within a 54,000-square-foot gated complex), the studios were rebuilt from the ground up by studio designer and architect Vincent Van Haaff, who incorporated new trends in gear and acoustics into its design (Van Haaff also worked on Capitol Studios). Artists who have recorded at Conway include Alicia Keys, Barbra Streisand, Foo Fighters, Stevie Wonder, and Dionne Warwick, who, Van Haaff has said, recorded the 1982 song, "That's What Friends Are For," by Dionne Warwick and Friends there while Michael Jackson and Elizabeth Taylor sat on a couch nearby.

Silent movie great Charlie Chaplin built what later became A&M Studios and is now Henson Recording Studios.

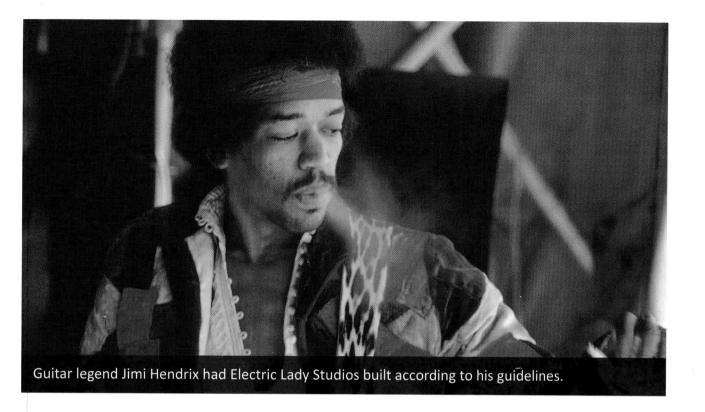
Guitar legend Jimi Hendrix had Electric Lady Studios built according to his guidelines.

ELECTRIC LADY STUDIOS, NEW YORK

Electric Lady Studios, located in New York City's Greenwich Village, was originally co-owned by Jimi Hendrix (at the time, label-owned-and-operated studios were the norm, and an artist-owned studio was a renegade concept). The building previously housed the popular Generation Club, and Hendrix and his manager Michael Jeffery planned to reopen the club, but decided instead to use the space as a recording studio. (Prior to the Generation Club, the building's basement contained The Village Barn from 1930 to 1967, a country-themed nightclub and dining hall.)

Designed by architect and acoustician John Storyk, Electric Lady Studios was designed to meet Hendrix's technical and aesthetic specifications, including round windows and theatrical lighting (Storyk made the walls white so they could be made any color with the right lighting). Construction of the studio took nearly double the amount of time

and money as planned, in part due to flooding attributed to Minetta Creek, an underground river. Although Hendrix spent only four weeks recording there before his death, the studio has since been used by many artists, including John Lennon, AC/DC, Bob Dylan, and The Strokes, whose 2013 album *Comedown Machine* was recorded there.

GANG RECORDING STUDIO, PARIS

In 1974, Claude Puterflam, one of the founding members of the French band Les Système Crapoutchik, founded Gang Recording Studio in the heart of Paris with sound engineer Jean Pierre Janiaud. The studio quickly became a major studio presence: *Starmania*, a French rock opera with music by Michel Berger and lyrics by Luc Plamondon, was recorded there in 1978. French composer, performer, and music producer Jean Michel Jarre and Grammy Award–winning French singer/songwriter Jean-Jacques Goldman have recorded there as well.

THE COLLABORATORS: PHARRELL WILLIAMS

In 2013, Pharrell Williams found himself at the crest of the disco-revival wave, lending his vocals to two of the summer's biggest smashes—the Marvin Gaye-inspired "Blurred Lines" by Robin Thicke (and featuring rapper T.I.), which Williams produced and co-wrote, and "Get Lucky," the song that finally allowed Daft Punk to crack major markets and garner mainstream airplay. Following a much-hyped leak, "Get Lucky" was released as a digital download in April 2013. Within a few months it soared to the Top 10 on music charts in more than thirty countries. The song was covered and recovered—including Internet versions that featured spliced clips of President Barack Obama "singing" "Get Lucky," and Williams' pitch-shifted vocals tweaked to sound like Michael Jackson.

Williams and Daft Punk—whom, Williams has said, are artists "not bound by time or space"—have collaborated before. As half of the renowned producing team, The Neptunes, which topped Billboard magazine's 2009 list of hottest producers of the decade, Williams has worked with artists ranging from

Pharrell Williams, who has worked with artists ranging from Miley Cyrus to Jay Z, lends his producing, writing, and singing talents to *Random Access Memories*.

Britney Spears and Limp Bizkit to Miley Cyrus and Jay Z. In 2003, he remixed "Harder, Better, Faster, Stronger" (a song that originally appeared on Daft Punk's *Discovery* album) for the French duo's 2003 remix album *Daft Club*. Daft Punk later served as co-writers and producers for the 2010 single "Hypnotize U" by N.E.R.D. (an acronym for "No-one Ever Really Dies"), a rock, funk, and hip-hop band Williams formed with Neptunes partner Chad Hugo and Shae Haley in 2000.

On *Random Access Memories*, Williams also co-wrote and contributed his vocals to the track "Lose Yourself to Dance," which is largely overshadowed by "Get Lucky," the making of which may go down in history as one of contemporary music's greatest cosmic coincidences. Williams, who saw Daft Punk at a Madonna party, expressed interest in working with the duo on their new record, even if that just meant he got "to play the tambourine." Soon, Williams met Daft Punk in their recording studio in Paris and, when asked what he was working on, mentioned he was in "a Nile Rodgers place." Unbeknownst to Williams, Bangalter and de Homem-Christo were already collaborating with Rodgers, the legendary Chic guitarist, on *Random Access Memories*. They played for him a track Rodgers had laid down that they wanted Williams to write to—a track that, with Williams's help, would arguably become the biggest song of any of their careers to date.

Although "Get Lucky" is about sex and love and having a good time—Williams has described it as the feeling of being on an exotic island before the sun comes up, where it's "forever four in the morning"—there seems to be a more substantive context at work. When Williams sings, "Like the legend of the phoenix" he invokes the famed bird of Greek mythology that is cyclically reborn, rising from the ashes of its former self to obtain new life. The line seems a metaphor for the cyclical nature of music, which can be dusted off and made new again—a theme that keeps with Daft Punk's desire to "give life back to music" throughout *Random Access Memories*.

Williams certainly has a knack for breathing life into a variety of industries—publishing (he is the author of *Pharrell: Places and Spaces I've Been*), fashion (his clothing lines include Billionaire Boys Club, ICECREAM, and i am OTHER), film (he scored 2013's *Despicable Me 2* after working on songs for the first film in 2010), and reality television (he's a mentor on the U.S. version of the fashion competition series *Styled to Rock*), just to name a few.

Perhaps it comes as no surprise, then, that the omnipresent Williams named his record label Star Trak and his son Rocket, and that he selected the image of an astronaut as the logo for his Billionaire Boys Club clothing line. Williams once said of Daft Punk that the only place for them to go from *Random Access Memories* is up, but he seems to be right there with them, out there like a shooting star, popping up in unexpected places to chart new and interesting courses. In "Get Lucky," when Williams sings, "So let's raise the bar and our cups to the stars," it's not only a collective celebration, but determination and a call to go where no man or music has gone before. And, cosmic coincidences aside, luck has very little to do with that.

RANDOM MEMORY

"It's crazy because, you know, on two sides of the Atlantic, we were both, like, in the same place—like, let's go back to that magical time where music and the liveliness of music is what moved people."

— Pharrell Williams on his collaboration with Daft Punk for the Creators Project video series

THE COLLABORATORS: PAUL WILLIAMS

On the surface, Paul Williams seems to be the unlikeliest collaborator on *Random Access Memories*. While the others have long careers in funk or rock or hip-hop, the seventy-three-year-old singer and songwriter is best known for penning some of the most popular love songs of the 1970s, including Helen Reddy's "You and Me Against the World," the Carpenters's "We've Only Just Begun" and "Rainy Days and Mondays," and "Evergreen" from the film *A Star Is Born,* starring Barbra Streisand, for which he won an Academy Award for Best Original Song.

During the 70s and 80s, Williams also made a variety of high-profile appearances in both film and television; his sweet-natured sense of humor made him a big hit on the talk show circuit. Perhaps his most famous film role was Little Enos Burdette in the Burt Reynolds–led *Smokey and the Bandit* films, but it was his turn as the villainous record producer, Swan, in Brian De Palma's 1974 cult film *Phantom of the Paradise* (which Williams co-scored and for which he received an Oscar nomination) that would land him on Daft Punk's radar. The film, a childhood favorite of both Thomas Bangalter and Guy-Manuel de Homem-Christo, was a rock musical based loosely upon an amalgamation of *The Phantom of the Opera, Faust,* and *The Picture of Dorian Gray*, and featured a helmet-wearing hero who sold his soul for rock and roll. The film, touted as a cinematic odyssey through the rock universe, would heavily influence Daft Punk's use of masks, disguises, and spectacle throughout the course of their careers.

Conversely, Williams—who stands 5'2"—has spent his entire life trying to get noticed. (Drug and alcohol addiction got the better of him during those early days, but Williams cleaned up his act in the 90s.) A self-described "fame addict," Williams has said that he respects artists like Daft Punk who express their craft without the hunger for public attention: "They disconnect who they are to allow you to experience what they create."

Singer/songwriter Paul Williams.

Williams, who is president and chairman of the board of the American Society of Composers, Authors and Publishers (ASCAP), has said one of the best things about working on *Random Access Memories* was the chance to record at his old stomping ground, the Henson Recording Studios, which is the site of the former A&M Studios. Back in the day, Williams worked closely with Jim Henson's Henson Productions on *The Muppet Movie* (he co-wrote the song "The Rainbow Connection") and other Muppet capers. He also served as a contract writer for A&M Records.

Williams co-wrote two songs for *Random Access Memories*: "Beyond" and "Touch," a tune on which he also serves as guest vocalist. Following a cinematic string introduction, "Beyond" settles into a smooth, slower-paced R&B groove that's reminiscent of Michael McDonald's 1982 single, "I Keep Forgettin' (Every Time You're Near)." The track lies in stark contrast to "Touch," a song Daft Punk considers the "core" of *Random Access Memories*, as well as its most complicated to date. Composed of 250 tracks, "Touch" is an auditory journey that runs for more than eight minutes and floats through genres, tones, tempos, and emotions, ranging from melodramatic to emotive and wistful. The track begins with Williams sounding like a theatrical ghoul—or phantom, as it were—before turning to a more sincere and hopeful tone.

If "this is a journey of the soul," as Daft Punk's vocoder-infused vocals sing on "Beyond," then Williams is baring his on *Random Access Memories*. When he sings, "Touch, where do you lead?/I need something more," it calls to mind not only a lover in search of affection, but also, perhaps, a songwriter in search of his muse. Williams has said that for guys known for techno, *Random Access Memories* is quite "elegant," and that he considers his participation in the making of the album a "gift," a chance not only to be relevant again, but to return to that vulnerable core, an honesty he expressed so eloquently in his sentimental love song days. If the central theme of *Random Access Memories* is to give life back to music, in doing so Daft Punk may have also induced a similar awakening for the long-dormant balladeer.

Paul Williams plays Swan, a villainous record producer, in Brian De Palma's *Phantom of the Paradise.*

THE COLLABORATORS: NILE RODGERS

It's hard to believe that Nile Rodgers, R&B's groove-meister and one of pop's most influential producers, was relatively proficient in classical instruments in his adolescence, but didn't even touch a guitar before the age of fifteen. That changed quickly when he began a career as a session guitarist in New York, touring with the Sesame Street Band at age nineteen, and joining the house band at Harlem's famous Apollo Theater the next year, where he played behind the likes of Screaming Jay Hawkins, Maxine Brown, Aretha Franklin, and Ben E. King. In 1970, Rodgers met bassist Bernard Edwards and together they formed The Big Apple Band, a group that backed the R&B act, New York City.

As the Big Apple Band, Rodgers and Edwards worked with recording artists Ashford & Simpson, Luther Vandross, and others, but because a New York artist named Walter Murphy had a band with the same name, Rodgers and Edwards were forced to change theirs to avoid confusion. In 1977, they formed

Nile Rodgers and his electric guitar, July 2013.

Chic, the renowned R&B group that would propel disco fever to new levels of popularity with songs such as "Le Freak"—Atlantic Records' only triple-platinum selling single—and "Good Times," a chart-topper that *Billboard* magazine named the number one R&B single of 1979, the same year the Sister Sledge dance hit "We Are Family," composed by Rodgers and Edwards, went Gold.

The 80s brought more accolades. In 1980, Rodgers and Edwards wrote and produced the album *Diana* for Diana Ross, which yielded the smash hits "Upside Down" and "I'm Coming Out." Chic's song "Good Times" became the bedrock of The Sugarhill Gang's "Rapper's Delight," the first multiplatinum hip-hop single. After Chic dissolved in 1983, Rodgers embarked on a successful solo career. He produced David Bowie's biggest-selling album *Let's Dance*—which included several hit singles, such as "China Girl," "Modern Love," and the title track "Let's Dance"—as well as the single "Original Sin" by INXS. Duran Duran worked extensively with Rodgers after he co-produced their highest-selling hit single "The Reflex" in 1983, which, incidentally,

was the same year Rodgers produced Madonna's blockbuster album, *Like a Virgin*. The list of hits and recognizable names goes on and on, and Rodgers continued collaborating into the 90s and 00s, a decade in which he focused on many soundtrack projects, films, and video games.

Daft Punk first met Rodgers at a New York listening party—Rodgers has said that virtually all of the recordings he's made are a result of impromptu meetings—for the duo's 1997 debut album *Homework* (Rodgers's Chic partner, Bernard Edwards, died the year prior). Thomas Bangalter and Guy-Manuel de Homem-Christo told Rodgers what an influence Chic had been on them. Although the artists expressed a desire to work together, a series of near-misses and scheduling conflicts delayed their collaboration until Daft Punk invited Rodgers to the *Random Access Memories* sessions at New York City's Electric Lady Studios—the very same studio, it turns out, where the first Chic single "Dance, Dance, Dance (Yowsah, Yowsah, Yowsah)" was recorded. (The studio had also been a nightclub in Rodgers's childhood neighborhood.)

Nile Rodgers co-produced Duran Duran's highest-selling hit single "The Reflex" in 1983.

Who better than Rodgers, the hit-maker himself, to help Daft Punk find their groove on an album that paid homage to the very music that Rodgers helped define? On *Random Access Memories*, Rodgers—who says Daft Punk was "cooler than I thought"—co-writes and plays his signature guitar riffs on three songs: "Give Life Back to Music," the album's mantra, which opens with a dramatic, all-instruments-in intro before settling into a gentle disco groove; "Lose Yourself to Dance," which combines Rodgers's catchy guitar hooks with Pharrell Williams's lighthearted vocals and, in contrast, Daft Punk's playful "c'mon, c'mon, c'mon" robot-vocals; and the lead, feel-good single "Get Lucky," which teams Rodgers, Williams, and Daft Punk once again.

Rodgers, who received the Winter Music Conference 2012 Lifetime Achievement Award at the 28th Annual Dance Music Awards in March 2013, calls the three songs he did on *Random Access Memories* as organic as anything he's ever done, and has hinted that he and the French music duo will collaborate again—this time, on some unreleased Chic material. Nearly twenty-five years after "Good Times," one of the most sampled songs in music history, it looks like happy days are, indeed, here again.

Nile Rodgers performs in England in 2013.

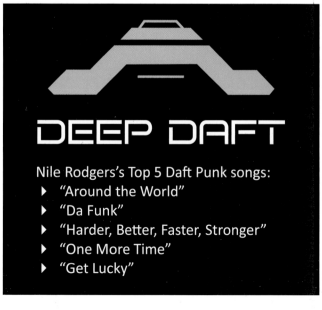

DEEP DAFT

Nile Rodgers's Top 5 Daft Punk songs:
- ▶ "Around the World"
- ▶ "Da Funk"
- ▶ "Harder, Better, Faster, Stronger"
- ▶ "One More Time"
- ▶ "Get Lucky"

THE COLLABORATORS: GIORGIO MORODER

It should come as no surprise that Daft Punk wanted to work with synth king Giorgio Moroder on *Random Access Memories*, since the iconic Italian producer is one of the duo's biggest influences and is considered the father of electronic disco.

Musical composer Giorgio Moroder in 1984.

Moroder appears on the song titled "Giorgio by Moroder"—a name which, Moroder has joked, sounds suitable for a fragrance—and simply performs a soliloquy about his life. He speaks of his yearning to become a musician and composer as a teen, how his devotion led him to sleep in his car near discotheques, and how he wanted to create music that reflected both what he had been hearing and what he had not. The latter of these desires led Moroder to the synthesizer, the machine that would come to define the musician's career.

Before Moroder hit it big with Donna Summer in the 70s—most notably with "Love to Love You Baby" and "I Feel Love"—he came to prominence in 1969 with the recording "Looky, Looky," a bubble-gum pop song that was released under the name "Giorgio." It was the song "Son of My Father," recorded in 1972, on which Moroder first used a synthesizer. Although older models had a habit of drifting out of tune, Moroder has said that anyone with a bit of talent and a lot of passion can use a synthesizer to create great music.

And that's just what Moroder did. With more than a hundred Gold and Platinum discs to his name, Moroder made his mark in a variety of musical genres and industries. In addition to his work with Summer, he produced electronic disco hits for The Three Degrees and Sparks, and has worked with an extensive roster of artists that includes Blondie (lead singer Debbie Harry supplied the lyrics to "Call Me," a song Moroder composed for the film *American Gigolo*), David Bowie, Van Halen, Pat Benatar, Cher, and Graham Nash, among others. He provided the score for a number of films, including 1978's *Midnight Express*, for which he won an Academy Award, and he later won two Best Song Oscars—for Irene Cara's "Flashdance . . . What a Feeling" from the film *Flashdance*, and Berlin's "Take My Breath Away" from *Top Gun*. (Moroder's influence was so great that when Hollywood composer Hans Zimmer built a new synthesizer to use on the film *The Dark Knight Rises*, he named it "Giorgio.") Moroder's techno-pop has

been sampled by countless pop, electronic, and rap artists, including Madonna, Lil Wayne, Fatboy Slim, DJ Shadow, and OutKast. As a producer, Moroder has said he is not one to linger on a song—his recordings with Donna Summer were reportedly done in hours—and he was impressed by the precision with which Daft Punk worked. For Moroder's contribution, the French duo set up several microphones in the recording studio, each one from a different era. When Moroder questioned the need for three mics, saying no one would hear the difference among them, the studio's engineer answered, "Thomas [Bangalter] will hear the difference." Moroder spoke into those mics for several hours and wasn't sure what Daft Punk would do with his contribution. He thought they might cut it up into a rap, but was pleased with the nine-minute tribute song that features snippets of his accent-tinged spoken history.

Legendary composer Giorgio Moroder.

118

Moroder feels that *Random Access Memories*—with its warm, full sound—is a step forward for dance music, which, in keeping with the *RAM* theme, he has said is in need of something new, something unobtainable by the mere push of a button. Although many consider Moroder a techno visionary, he had no idea what an influence his computer compositions would have on the music industry. As he says on "Giorgio by Moroder," "Once you free your mind about the concept of harmony and of music being correct, you can do whatever you want." Without realizing it, Moroder's playful mixing of Moogs, memory banks, and music created a model for generations of composers and producers to come. These days, the seventy-three-year-old musician is back in the studio.

DEEP DAFT

Some say Daft Punk's enigmatic image was inspired in part by Giorgio Moroder, who, for much of his career, hid his face behind black sunglasses and a bushy black mustache. What's more, the cover of Moroder's digitally-recorded, vocoder-heavy 1979 solo album *E=MC²* shows him holding open a *Saturday Night Fever*–esque white jacket and revealing a robot torso of dials and knobs—a visual synthesis of macho man and machine.

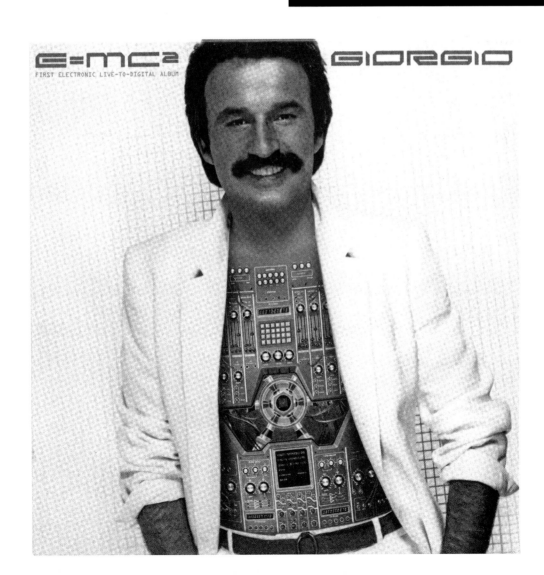

THE COLLABORATORS:
PANDA BEAR

Noah Lennox, better known as Panda Bear, is a founding member of the band Animal Collective. He first heard Daft Punk's seductive steady bassline and talk box vocoder-processed sound on MTV late one night in the 90s, when he caught the video for "Around the World," the dance chart-topper from the duo's debut album *Homework*.

Entranced by what he has called the "ritualness" of electronic music, Lennox called *Homework* one of the few albums he and his older brother could agree upon for road-trip music in his youth, and the driving rhythms would leave an imprint on the young musician as he went on to form Animal Collective.

Music group Animal Collective in New York, October 2007: (left to right) Dave Portner (Avey Tare), Noah Lennox (Panda Bear), Brian Weitz (Geologist), and Josh Dibb (Deakin).

Experimental in nature, Animal Collective is one of those groups that can be difficult to pin down. The band has been classified as psych folk or noise rock, but, at heart, they're basically a group of guys who like to try new things stylistically from album to album—not unlike Daft Punk themselves. The similarities extend to both groups' use of *persona* as a way to focus attention on the music rather than the men behind it. In addition to the members' monikers (Avey Tare, Deakin, and Geologist, in addition to Panda Bear), Animal Collective, in its early days, wore makeup and masks that would become a prominent characteristic of the group's live performances.

Interested in working with Daft Punk, Lennox approached the duo about doing a remix of an Animal Collective song (they turned him down) and, later, for one of his solo songs (he was turned down again). However, a year and a half after Lennox's second request, they asked him to come to their Paris studio. The result of that invite turned out to be a vocal turn for Lennox on the penultimate track of *Random Access Memories* titled "Doin' It Right," a song that the duo has referred to as the only purely electronic piece on the album with a modern style. Lennox's earnest croon against Daft Punk's digital blueprint creates the fascinating marriage of contrast and surprise that has come to define Daft Punk's fourth studio album as a whole.

Panda Bear performing at The Bowery Ballroom in New York.

Lennox and Daft Punk wound up cutting the record in just three days—an unusually short amount of time for the instinctively nomadic Lennox, who likes to spend time with a piece of music and was nervous about having to come up with something creative on the spot. Still, Daft Punk gave him free rein within that short span, encouraging him to "do something good." That something good came near the very end of the third day, almost by surprise, and had the duo—and now millions around the world—nodding their heads in approval.

THE COLLABORATORS: JULIAN CASABLANCAS

Daft Punk's demo, "Instant Crush," was gathering dust. As the story goes, the duo played it for Julian Casablancas, the front man of the indie rock band, The Strokes, one of the duo's contemporary rock favorites. The two clicked and the song became the fifth track on *Random Access Memories.*

"Instant Crush" is a mid-tempo groove on which Casablancas handles the vocals and lead guitar (he also served as co-writer and co-producer). The tune feels like a bridge, not only in its placement on *Random Access Memories*, where it sits between the inconspicuous "Within" and the booty-shaking "Lose Yourself to Dance," but also in its composition. It opens with rhythmic guitar chugs that call to mind the 1982 hit song "Eye in the Sky" by the Alan Parsons Project, features a guitar solo, and ends with what sounds like a lively nod to "Pop Muzik," the 1979 chart-topper by new wave pioneer, M (Robin Scott). The song also features Casablancas's processed and uncharacteristically high-register vocals—a singing style that Guy-Manuel de Homem-Christo has said is simply the way Casablancas reacted to the track. Casablancas also experimented with soft falsetto vocals—in lieu of his iconic full-throttle warble—on The Strokes' fifth studio album, *Comedown Machine*, which was released just months before *Random Access Memories*.

The Strokes—consisting of Nick Valensi, Albert Hammond Jr., Nikolai Fraiture, and Fabrizio Moretti, in addition to Casablancas—blasted onto the music scene with their 2001 debut album *Is This It*, which was both a critical and commercial success, and helped put garage rock back on the map. In contrast, Casablancas's 2009 solo album *Phrazes for the Young* (the title of which was inspired by the Oscar Wilde book, *Phrases and Philosophies for the Use of the Young*) is strongly influenced by new wave and electronica. Unlike much of The Strokes' music, Casablancas features more synth-based songs on *Phrazes*—"It can be hard to experiment when you're in a band," he has said—and wanted to bridge the gap between

Julian Casablancas, November 2009.

traditional and modern music, not unlike Daft Punk, for whom experimentation is a core tenet.

Also like the French duo, Casablancas seems to have a bit of a playful, commercial side, as evidenced by some of his side projects. In 2008, he worked with fellow *RAM* collaborator Pharrell Williams and singer-songwriter Santigold on the single "My Drive Thru," a song produced by The Neptunes for Converse's centennial "Three Artists. One Song" campaign. In 2009, he recorded "Boombox" with *Saturday Night Live (SNL)* alums Andy Samberg, Jorma Taccone, and Akiva Schaffer (aka, the comedy troupe The Lonely Island), as well as "I Wish It Was Christmas Today," which was based on a popular *SNL* skit by Jimmy Fallon, Horatio Sanz, Chris Kattan, and Tracy Morgan.

With the way they both explore pop culture and the boundaries of music, perhaps it was inevitable that Daft Punk and Casablancas would eventually come together on a song. As Casablancas sings on "Instant Crush," "A little time with you is all that I get/That's all we make because it's all we can take." Sometimes the biggest impacts are a result of the briefest encounters.

Julian Casablancas with The Strokes in Benicássim, Spain.

THE COLLABORATORS: TODD EDWARDS

House music producer Todd Edwards is known for his complex vocal sampling, or his "musical collages," as he describes his instantly recognizable style—tiny dots and chirps of sound in different tempos and keys that are laced together into a delirious whole. The technique is credited with giving birth to the UK garage style of dance music, and earned him the nickname "Todd the God."

Inspired by Marc Kinchen (better known as house producer MK) as well as everything from disco and pop to soundtrack and orchestral music, Edwards has been producing for twenty years, and his remixes number in the hundreds. Edwards worked with Daft Punk on their 2001 album *Discovery,* co-writing (his writing credit is listed as Todd Imperatrice), co-producing, and providing vocals for the song "Face to Face." Ever since, fans have been asking if he would collaborate with the duo again. Since Daft Punk is renowned for exploring new challenges, Edwards didn't know if he'd be asked . . . but he was. The second time around, Daft Punk played him a gospel-y, Doobie-Brothers-sounding track, on which they wanted Edwards to sing for *Random Access Memories*. Although Edwards shied away from singing early in his career (his vocal turn on *Discovery* was an exception to the rule), Bangalter encouraged him to focus on his songwriting and vocals, suggesting that he could find new audiences for both acts from working on the new album.

While "Face to Face" sent Edwards to Paris, this time he worked with Daft Punk in the Henson Recording Studios in Los Angeles, singing into the same microphone that Frank Sinatra once used. The duo asked Edwards to channel a West Coast vibe—a confounding request for the New Jersey native, who had only been to LA a couple

On Todd Edwards's tracks for Daft Punk, he used the same microphone as Frank Sinatra.

of times (Edwards was also new to recording live instrumentation). However, inspired by LA's glorious weather and vibe, Edwards worked with Bangalter to write the song and also provided his signature "cut-ups," or decoupage house stylings, which Daft Punk used as the track's chorus. The result is the light, polished, and super-smooth "Fragments of Time," a song that Edwards co-produced. The tune showcases how his style can fit into a genre other than house or club, an aspect he intends to explore as his career progresses.

Edwards was so inspired by the time he spent in LA, driving from Bangalter's house with the top down in the bright sunshine and working with Daft Punk for those three weeks on *Random Access Memories,* that the song became a way to remember and relive those moments: "I'll just keep playing back." Edwards has said his time with the duo made living in Jersey feel as if he had been making "music in a bubble," spending most of the last fifteen years cooped up in a room (ironically, Edwards was never really a part of the club scene his music invigorated). In the end, he decided to pack up his studio and drove a fourteen-foot truck across the country to Los Angeles, which he currently calls home. On "Fragments of Time," Edwards croons, "I don't ever want it to end." Now it doesn't have to.

Todd Edwards.

THE COLLABORATORS: CHILLY GONZALES

For a guy who isn't all that fond of collaborating, Chilly Gonzales, the classically trained pianist-cum-rap artist known for his convention-shattering career, has quite the collaborative track record. Citing exceptions for artists who are "in possession of some true key to the zeitgeist," Gonzales has worked regularly with electro-punk bad girl Peaches and singer-songwriter Feist. He also lent a helping hand to the harmony department on Daft Punk's *Random Access Memories*.

Although Gonzales appears on two tracks—playing keyboards on "Give Life Back to Music" and on solo piano for "Within," which he co-wrote—he has said it was his "mathematics of music" that brought him and the duo together. On "Within," Daft Punk tasked Gonzales with composing a section of music that bridged a shift from A minor, the key of the album's first three songs, to B-flat minor for the next block of tracks (Gonzales identified the common chord of F major to do the trick).

Transitions are nothing new to the multifaceted Gonzales, whose career has evolved through several incarnations over the past twenty years. Although he was trained as a pianist, in the 1990s he embarked on an indie rock career as the leader of the alternative band, Son. After a few albums, Gonzales parted ways with his Canadian record label and went off to Europe, where he developed a hip-hop career with German record label Kitty-Yo, releasing several albums, including *The Entertainist*, his first rap LP. He returned to his pianist roots in 2004 with *Solo Piano*, a stripped-down instrumental album and his best selling to date (he released the follow-up *Solo Piano II* in 2012). He mixed it up with some 70s soft-rock-inspired fare on 2008's *Soft Power* and changed gears again on 2010's *Ivory Tower* (Gonzales also produced, co-wrote, and starred in the accompanying film of the same name), for which he worked with Boys Noize, a German electro music producer and DJ. That effort was followed by *The Unspeakable Chilly Gonzales*, which was released in 2011 and billed as the "world's first orchestral rap album."

Chilly Gonzales holds the world record for the longest solo-artist concert performance.

Chilly Gonzales.

Not surprisingly, Gonzales (born Jason Beck, but nicknamed Gonzo) has a sense of humor as striking and varied as his music—he has been known to perform in a bathrobe and slippers—and seems to revel in contradiction. The once self-proclaimed "King of the Berlin Underground" (he is a member of the Berlin-based hip-hop band Puppetmastaz, a rap group consisting of puppets), Gonzales holds a world record for the longest solo-artist concert performance. At a Paris theater in 2009, he played the piano continuously and without repetition— "I will break the record without sounding like a broken record"—for twenty-seven hours, three minutes, and forty-four seconds (incidentally, his song "Never Stop" was the opening piano tune featured on Apple's original iPad commercials). Later that year, he famously challenged fellow avant-pop auteur and solo pianist Andrew W.K. to a piano battle at Joe's Pub in New York City, saying, "Let's give them something to talk about."

If there's one thing Gonzales has learned throughout his career, it's that pop success is as much about buzz as it is about breadth of talent. So when the robots croon, "I need to know now/Please tell me who I am" on the *RAM* track "Within," one gets the impression that the versatile Gonzales—pianist, producer, and prankster—already knows.

THE COLLABORATORS:
DJ FALCON

Of all the collaborators on *Random Access Memories*, Stéphane Quême's (otherwise known as DJ Falcon) ties with Daft Punk run the deepest. The French DJ and record producer met Thomas Bangalter and Guy-Manuel de Homem-Christo through his friend Pedro Winter (also known as Busy P), the head of Ed Banger Records and Daft Punk's former manager. As teens, Quême and Winter hung out and skateboarded together, a pastime which earned Quême the skater nickname of "Bob." In 1993, when Daft Punk was just beginning work on their first studio album *Homework*, Winter organized a big party in Paris. It was there that he introduced Bangalter and de Homem-Christo to "Bob." The guys struck up a friendship, particularly Quême and Bangalter, who would also develop a professional relationship.

After working in the A&R (Artist & Repertoire) Department at Virgin Records, Quême released his first LP, *Hello My Name Is DJ Falcon*, on Bangalter's label Roulé in 1999. Since their birthdays were only a day apart (Quême was born on January 2, Bangalter on January 3), Bangalter thought it best to work on the track between those two days. "That's just typical Thomas," Quême has said, noting that Bangalter looks for "the special moment" in everything he does. In 1999, Quême also produced a popular remix

DJ Falcon, aka Stéphane Quême.

of "La Mouche" by Cassius, the veteran French house music duo. The following year, Quême and Bangalter formed the band Together, releasing two singles ("So Much Love to Give" and the eponymous "Together") with Roulé.

On *Random Access Memories*, Quême co-produces and plays the modular synthesizer on the closing track "Contact," which was actually a demo he and Bangalter did years ago; an early version of the song is featured on a recording of a 2002 DJ set at Amsterdam's Paradiso by Bangalter, Cassius, and Quême. With its synth-organs and use of sampling (the only track on *RAM* that includes this element), "Contact" is considered the most old-school Daft Punk piece on the album.

Daft Punk and Quême thought "Contact" was in need of an element akin to a countdown, and Bangalter had the idea to contact NASA, which gave Daft Punk access to all of its mission recordings from which to sample. While choosing one to use, Bangalter heard Captain Eugene Cernan of Apollo 17 mention the name "Bob," Quême's nickname. It was another one of those special moments, and the sample was decisively added to the track.

Quême, whose DJ sets are inspired by everything from electro and house classics to indie dance and new rave, hasn't released any original music aside from "Contact" in more than ten years, during which time he traveled the world as a photographer and DJ, and toured with artists such as The Chemical Brothers and Daft Punk. (A special edition of Daft Punk's *Alive 2007* album features a book containing tour photographs taken by Quême.) He also got back into the remix game in 2012 with Justice's "New Lands," Alan Braxe's "Time Machine," and Alex Gopher's "Hello Inc." Quême has said that "it's really cool" to see Daft Punk's work come full circle—just as he and the duo have sampled records, so can today's musicians sample *Random Access Memories*. With plans to return to the studio to work on original material, Quême might just be one of them.

DJ Falcon co-produced the *Random Access Memories* closing track "Contact."

DEEP DAFT

"Hey, Bob, I'm looking at what Jack was talking about, and it's definitely not a particle that's nearby. It is a bright object, and it's obviously rotating because it's flashing. It's way out in the distance, certainly rotating in a very rhythmic fashion, because the flashes come around almost on time. As we look back at the earth, it's up at about eleven o'clock, about maybe ten or twelve Earth diameters. I don't know whether that does you any good, but there's something out there."

—Captain Eugene Cernan, Apollo 17, as heard on "Contact."

THE COLLABORATORS:
JOHN "JR" ROBINSON AND OMAR HAKIM

When the members of Daft Punk set out to create music using drums rather than drum machines, they called upon two of the industry's most seasoned drummers: John "JR" Robinson and Omar Hakim. Robinson and Hakim practically split the drumming duties on *Random Access Memories* right down the middle—Robinson appears on the first six tracks, and Hakim takes care of six of the last seven, also joining Robinson on "Giorgio by Moroder." ("Doin' It Right" is the only song to have its steady drum beat entirely synth-provided.)

John "JR" Robinson giving a master class and clinic in drumming.

A prolific studio drummer who is considered the most recorded drummer in history, Robinson is most known for his work with Quincy Jones and Michael Jackson, including the multiplatinum *Off the Wall* album, and the charity single smash-hit, "We Are the World." His discography includes some of pop music's biggest hits, including Rufus and Chaka Khan's "Ain't Nobody," which won a Grammy Award in 1984; Lionel Richie's "All Night Long (All Night)," a number-one single; and Wilson Phillips's chart-toppers "Hold On," "Release Me," and "You're in Love." He has worked with many recording artists, including Madonna, Eric Clapton, The Pointer Sisters, David Lee Roth, and Barbra Streisand, with whom he recently toured. Robinson has two solo albums, 2004's *Funkshui* and *Platinum*, released in 2010. In 2013, he joined legendary rock drummers (such as Sheila E. and Jason Bonham) and fellow *Random Access Memories* collaborator Pharrell Williams to provide percussion for Hans Zimmer's soundtrack for the film *Man of Steel*.

John "JR" Robinson.

Hakim, who began playing the drums at age five and performed publicly with his father Hasan Hakim, who played trombone for Duke Ellington and Count Basie, has been a drummer and session man for more than thirty-five years. Crediting jazz vibraphonist Mike Mainieri with giving him his first break in 1980 when he was hired to play in Carly Simon's touring band, Hakim was a member of Weather Report, a jazz fusion band of the 70s and early 80s; has played high-tech V-drums for Madonna as well as acoustic drums with the Hank Jones Great Jazz Trio; and has worked with Sting (Hakim appeared in the 1985 rockumentary *Bring On the Night*, performing one of the most renowned drum solos ever captured on film), Anita Baker, Bruce Springsteen, Mariah Carey, David Bowie, Miles Davis, Chic, Bobby McFerrin, and many others. In 1989, he produced and released his first solo album, *Rhythm Deep*, which earned him his first Grammy nomination, and in the 90s he toured with Lionel Ritchie and Madonna for eight years.

Omar Hakim.

Omar Hakim's drumming breathes new life into the tracks on *Random Access Memories*.

Thomas Bangalter has said that, while working on "Giorgio by Moroder," he hummed a complicated drum beat to Hakim, who instantly replicated and enhanced it, leaving the French musician—whose experience to date with Daft Punk and as a solo artist had been mostly with electronic drumming—to wonder, "What have we been missing?" What, indeed.

Quinn.

DEEP DAFT

Quinn, a recording artist and drummer with nine solo CDs to his credit, lent a hand on percussion on *Random Access Memories*; his contributions can be heard throughout the album. Quinn, who has said that making electronic sounds organically is the thing he enjoys most, brought every drum he owned to the Daft Punk sessions at Conway Recording Studios in Los Angeles, jumping back and forth between his drum kits and a whole table of percussion to put down flavorings that complemented the grooves of Hakim and Robinson.

THE CHART-TOPPER

Random Access Memories, with its host of collaborators and studio performance artistry, hit the #1 spot on digital charts in ninety-seven countries, dominated UK charts to become the fastest-selling album of 2013, and had the biggest first-week album sales in France (going triple-Platinum) since 2007. The album's release not only earned Daft Punk its first #1 album in countries such as the United States, Germany, Australia, and Japan, but the vinyl version became the biggest selling vinyl album in SoundScan's LP vinyl chart history, selling an impressive 339,000 copies in the U.S. alone in the first week.

In addition to unprecedented album sales, a steady stream of critical acclaim arrived from media outlets across the globe, including *Rolling Stone* ("Its brilliance is often irrefutable "), *Entertainment Weekly* ("a bravura live performance that stands out against pro forma knob-twiddling"), *The Guardian* ("It felt like a major event before its release: more incredibly, it still does once you've heard it."), Vh1 India ("it might just save music again "), and *Pitchfork* ("By the time you make it to the album's astonishing final stretch, it's hard not to think that Daft Punk have succeeded at what they set out to do.").

RANDOM ACCESS MEMORIES AROUND THE WORLD

Chart	Peak Position
Australian Albums Chart	1
Austrian Albums Chart	1
Belgian Albums Chart (Flanders)	1
Belgian Albums Chart (Wallonia)	1
Canadian Albums Chart	1
Croatian Albums Chart	6
Czech Albums Chart	1
Danish Albums Chart	1
Dutch Albums Chart	2
Estonian Albums Chart	4
Finnish Albums Chart	1
French Albums Chart	1
German Albums Chart	1
Greek Albums Chart	3
Hungarian Albums Chart	1
Irish Albums Chart	1
Italian Albums Chart	1
Japanese Albums Chart	3
Mexican Albums Chart	1
New Zealand Albums Chart	1
Norwegian Albums Chart	1
Polish Albums Chart	4
Portuguese Albums Chart	1
Russian Albums Chart	1
Scottish Albums Chart	1
South Korean Albums Chart	8
Slovenian Albums Chart	7
Spanish Albums Chart	1
Swedish Albums Chart	2
Swiss Albums Chart	1
UK Albums Chart	1
US Billboard 200	1
US Dance/Electronic Albums	1

THE PHENOMENON

Buoyed by *Random Access Memories'* critical and chart performance, Daft Punk saw its popularity skyrocket in 2013. Whereas before they were known mostly in electronic dance circles and within the pages of music journalism, with their fourth studio album Thomas Bangalter and Guy-Manuel de Homem-Christo reached the kind of mainstream success that was leaps and bounds beyond anything their previous work in music or film had garnered.

Although perhaps inconceivable to the duo's fans of twenty years, plenty of folks out there had never heard of Daft Punk until their helmet-clad heads began showing up in unlikely places. Besides gracing music magazine covers—from *Rolling Stone, Q Magazine,* and *Vibe*—Daft Punk appeared in fashion shoots for *Vogue* and *CR Fashion Book* and had the Internet bristling with all kinds of robot sightings and rumors, including the premiere of a brand of "Get Lucky" condoms (not true), another line of action figures (true, see page 137), and a Daft Punk racecar (partially true). In March 2013, Columbia Records, Daft Punk's label, entered a partnership deal with the British Formula One racing team Lotus, which raced in a specially branded car emblazoned with the duo's logo. In May of that year, Daft Punk made a rare public appearance at the 2013 Monaco Grand Prix to support Lotus F1, and wore the team's racing overalls to walk drivers Kimi Räikkönen and Romain Grosjean to the grid. Daft Punk is also featured in a thirty-second commercial for Lotus F1 that was directed by the renowned music video director Jonas Åkerlund.

As the mega-hit "Get Lucky" continued its reign over the summer music charts, securing airplay across seven different formats of radio, Daft Punk joined the elite of pop faves whose songs were topping Top 40 airplay, such as Bruno Mars, Miley Cyrus, and Macklemore. The duo's seeming ubiquity gained the attention of popular late night talk show host Stephen Colbert, whose decision to invite Daft Punk on the show sparked a world-famous hissy fit that intensified the duo's already heavy media coverage.

On August 6, 2013, Daft Punk was scheduled to appear exclusively on an episode of Comedy Central's satirical late night series, The Colbert Report, that was heralded as "StePhest Colbchella '013: The Song of the Summer of the Century." News of Daft Punk's appearance (the duo's first ever on late night) ricocheted across the Internet, prompted, in part, by Colbert's mysterious cameo the week before on Late Night with Jimmy Fallon, where he emerged on stage dancing to "Get Lucky."

However, when viewers tuned into The Colbert Report on August 6, Daft Punk was nowhere to be found. Hours before the show's taping, the appearance was reportedly canceled due to contractual obligations having to do with the upcoming MTV Video Music Awards (VMAs) set to air later that month on Comedy Central's sister station, MTV (whether Daft Punk or MTV officially pulled the plug is still not completely clear). Without the dynamic French duo, the resulting Colbert program, instead, became a rant-filled twenty-two minutes in which the scorned Colbert waffled between temper tantrum and confessional.

In Daft Punk's place, the program featured Robin Thicke singing "Blurred Lines," a song that Colbert would deem "for personal and professional reasons" (and to some quite accurately) as the song of the summer. Additionally, a "Get Lucky" montage music video—that would soon go viral—featured Colbert dancing with Hugh Laurie, Jeff Bridges, Bryan Cranston, Jon Stewart,

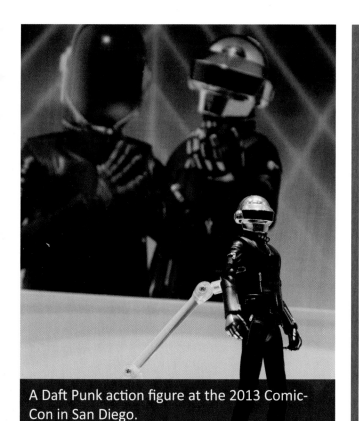

A Daft Punk action figure at the 2013 Comic-Con in San Diego.

PRETTY IN PUNK

In 2013, Daft Punk was turned into action figures once again. The latest limited edition, high-end action figures were part of Japanese toy company S. H. Figuarts's advanced series from Bandai Japan's premium collector's label, Tamashii Nations. Standing just under six inches, the figures, which were created under the supervision of Daft Punk, featured seven sets of left/right interchangeable hand parts for "dynamic posing." First glimpsed during the San Diego Comic-Con in July, the action figures were made available in North America in December 2013 at a retail price of approximately $45.

Matt Damon (dancing in The Matt Damon Booth), the high-kicking Radio City Rockettes, and Fallon (on the aforementioned clip), on the *America's Got Talent* stage and in the office of Henry Kissinger, who comically threatened to call security. Some, including music site *Pitchfork*, speculated that the Daft Punk incident was an elaborate stunt to promote the upcoming *VMAs,* considering the appearance of the actors and Robin Thicke was prerecorded. (Colbert later explained that since Daft Punk hadn't intended to sing or speak, he needed to pre-plan some elements of the show.) In the end, the hoopla surrounding the Daft Punk no-show was arguably just as effective in generating publicity for the duo's profile as an in-studio interview or performance would have been.

After Colbert spilled the beans about Daft Punk's upcoming *VMA* appearance, anticipation began building in the weeks leading up to the awards show. Finally, on August 29, Daft Punk took the stage at Brooklyn's Barclays Center alongside collaborators Nile Rodgers and Pharrell Williams, where they served (a bit anticlimactically, considering the *Colbert* fallout) as presenters, rather than performers. The only Daft Punk music came during a brief music video for "Lose Yourself to Dance," the second single from *Random Access Memories*, which appeared during a commercial break in the same way "Get Lucky" was heralded on *Saturday Night Live* months before.

Robin Thicke wears some sharp lines here, but he sang his hit "Blurred Lines" when Daft Punk didn't appear on *The Colbert Report*.

ROBO OP

In July 2013, midtown Manhattan sightings of Daft Punk began popping up on YouTube, Instagram, and other social media sites, showing the duo drawing crowds and stopping traffic while posing with fashion model Karlie Koss. It was later learned that the three were part of a photo shoot for a fashion spread in the August issue of *Vogue*.

FREESTYLE

In September 2013, Currys, a UK electronics and appliance retailer, made news after it was reported that one of the chain's stores broke up job applicants into teams and had them participate in a dance-off in order to compete for a position, with at least one applicant dancing to Daft Punk's "Around the World." Currys later apologized for the incident and invited all the applicants for another interview.

Nile Rodgers.

ROBO OP

For a cover story titled "Revenge of the Nerds," Daft Punk, dressed in blinged out Yves Saint Laurent Le Smoking tuxedos, joined *Random Access Memories* collaborator Pharrell Williams on the cover of *Vibe* magazine's summer issue.

PRETTY IN PUNK

In August 2013, actress Milla Jovovich joined Daft Punk for a photo spread in *CR Fashion Book*, for which the French duo sported their signature Yves Saint Laurent suits (Jovovich was said to wear the same Saint Laurent duds previously worn by Lady Gaga and Kate Moss). The photos were intended as both a digital love story and a celebration of the mega-success of *Random Access Memories.*

RANDOM MEMORY

"The ['Lose Yourself to Dance'] video came about like this: 'Hey Nile, what are you doing?' 'I'm in Europe.' 'Can you get over here and do a music video?' 'Sure, OK, cool.' It was that simple. . . . We had such a great time making the record that we bonded in such a way that's probably, you know, a lifelong bond. So doing the video was nothing It was my pleasure and honor to do it."

—Nile Rodgers to *MTV News* backstage at the 2013 *VMAs*

THE DAFT PUNK
INFLUENCE

With four studio albums, one soundtrack, and other various productions and remixes to their credit, Daft Punk has helped shape the music scene. From "Da Funk" to "Get Lucky," their music catalog has influenced producers, DJs, and other music makers who continue to sample or recreate their chants, grooves, funks, drums, and synth rhythms into a variety of new forms.

Kanye West at the 2008 Grammy Awards.

Song	Artist	Year	Daft Punk Sample/ Inspiration
"09:00 – Daft Purple"	The Kleptones	2006	"Harder, Better, Faster, Stronger"; "Technologic"
"10.20.Life"	Reconcile	2012	"The Son of Flynn"
"Aerodynamit Punx"	Mr. Kill	2007	"Aerodynamic"
"Around the World"	Kou Chou Ching	2010	"Around the World"
"Around the World"	Termanology (featuring Boogz Boogetz and Kali Raps)	2013	"Around the World"
"At the Bar"	Diamond (featuring Jackie Chain and Juicy)	2012	"One More Time"
"Based God Fucked My Bitches"	Lil B	2012	"One More Time"
"Beautiful Light"	Uppermost	2012	"Face to Face"
"Been Thru This"	Ivana Santilli	2008	"Face to Face"
"Believe"	Cher	1998	"Revolution 909"
"Bomb First (My Second Reply)"	Makaveli	1996	"Da Funk"
"Boom Boom Pow"	Black-Eyed Peas	2009	"Harder, Better, Faster, Stronger"
"The Boys"	Nicki Minaj and Cassie	2012	"Technologic"
"Clap Your Daft Punk"	CMC & Silenta	2012	"Harder, Better, Faster, Stronger"

DEEP DAFT

Kanye West performed his song "Stronger," which features a vocal sample of Daft Punk's "Harder, Better, Faster, Stronger," at the 2008 Grammy Awards at Los Angeles's Staples Center with a surprise guest . . . Daft Punk. In the first-ever television appearance of their careers, Daft Punk appeared atop their trademark pyramid to accompany West on an original version of "Stronger" that was created specifically for the evening. Although West and Daft Punk did not collaborate in the studio (the actors who portray the robots in the film *Daft Punk's Electroma* served as stand-ins for the "Stronger" video), Thomas Bangalter and Guy-Manuel de Homem-Christo have said they were pleased with how West's track turned out when they heard it for the first time on a Los Angeles radio station while waiting for a flight to San Francisco. "The vibe of the music we do separately connected," de Homem-Christo has said. In 2013, Daft Punk co-produced four songs on West's sixth studio album, *Yeezus*.

Song	Artist	Year	Daft Punk Sample/ Inspiration
"Come Again"	The Kleptones	2010	"Robot Rock"
"Cowboy George"	The Fall	2010	"Harder, Better, Faster, Stronger"
"Daft Cant"	Hellfish (featuring The DJ Producer)	2006	"Aerodynamic"
"Daft Punk Is Playing at My House (Soulwax Shibuya Mix)"	LCD Soundsystem	2005	"Harder, Better, Faster, Stronger"; "Digital Love"; "Burnin'"; "Oh Yeah"; "Rollin' & Scratchin'"; "Teachers"; "Rock 'n Roll"
"Daft Punk Rave"	Zomby	2008	"Technologic (Peaches No Logic Remix)"
"Daft Sound"	Afrojack	2010	"Technologic"
"Dare"	Gorillaz (featuring Shawn Ryder)	2005	"Revolution 909"
"Deaf Junk (Never Over)"	Aschvault	2008	"Harder, Better, Faster, Stronger"; "Aerodynamic"
"Dixit"	Uppermost	2011	"Harder, Better, Faster, Stronger"; "Da Funk"; "Digital Love"; "Robot Rock"; "Around the World"; "Superheroes"; "Too Long"; "The Prime Time of Your Life"; "Fresh"
"Down the Road"	C2C	2012	"Around the World"
"Dream Big"	Jazmine Sullivan	2001	"Veridis Quo"
"Du"	Cro	2012	"Something About Us"
"Electricity"	The Avalanches	1999	"Da Funk"
"Electrocution"	Front Line Assembly	1997	"Rollin' & Scratchin'"
"Flow"	Uppermost	2012	"Digital Love"; "Something About Us"
"The Game Has Changed"	Pharrell	2010	"The Game Has Changed"
"Geekin'"	will.i.am	2013	"Technologic"
"Get It Get It"	Girl Talk	2010	"One More Time"; "Digital Love"
"Giallo"	LBCK	2009	"Human After All"

Song	Artist	Year	Daft Punk Sample/ Inspiration
"Give Me a Beat"	Girl Talk	2008	"Face to Face"
"Good Morning"	Wes Nyle (featuring Young Sam)	2011	"One More Time"
"Good to Know You'll Be There"	Renard	2010	"Harder, Better, Faster, Stronger"
"Groove for Life"	Todd Terry	2002	"Burnin'"
"Gum"	She (2)	2009	"Oh Yeah"
"Harder"	Drumsound & Bassline Smith	2007	"Harder, Better, Faster, Stronger"
"HeartBreaker"	Teriyaki Boyz	2005	"Human After All"
"Highlife (WBBL Remix)"	WBBL	2011	"High Life"
"Hipster Girls"	Lil B	2010	"High Fidelity"
"Hot Box"	Hatiras	2005	"Burnin'"
"Hypnomatic"	Joey Riot	2006	"Technologic"
"I Got It From My Mama (Video Remix)"	will.i.am (featuring The Paradiso Girls)	2007	"Around the World"
"Insane"	Dark Monks	2002	"Burnin'"
"International Track"	Drop Out Orchestra	2011	"Around the World"
"Intronection"	Etienne De Crécy	2000	"Ouverture"
"The Joker"	Pacewon and Mr. Green	2008	"Aerodynamic"
"Just Like Old Times"	The Phantom's Revenge	2008	"On/Off"
"Kingstonlogic"	Terry Lynn	2009	"Technologic"
"Laatste Keer"	The Opposites	2013	"Get Lucky"
"Less Go Over Werk It"	Overwerk	2010	"Harder, Better, Faster, Stronger"
"Let Me See You"	Girl Talk	2008	"Harder, Better, Faster, Stronger"
"Love Me After 12 A.M."	M-Flo (featuring Alex)	2007	"Digital Love"
"LTFU (One More Time)"	Machine Gun Kelly	2011	"One More Time"
"Made the Change"	Craig G and Marley Marl	2008	"One More Time"
"Make It Faster"	Cruz and the White	2004	"Harder, Better, Faster, Stronger"; "Aerodynamic"
"Make Some Room vs Technologic (CZT's Astounding and Standing High Bootleg)"	Cazzette	2012	"Technologic"
"My Groove"	Rain (2) (featuring Epik High)	2004	"High Life"

Song	Artist	Year	Daft Punk Sample/ Inspiration
"The New Science"	Kids and Explosions	2010	"Da Funk"
"The Norm"	Uppermost	2012	"Around the World"
"On and On"	Girl Talk	2010	"Television Rules the Nation"
"One Mo' Gin"	Play-N-Skillz (featuring Lil Jon, Krayzie Bone and Bun B)	2008	"One More Time"
"One More Time"	Bulu	2010	"One More Time"
"One More Time"	Cut & Run	2007	"One More Time"; "Aerodynamic"
"One More Time"	Sonnie Carson (featuring Emilio Rojas)	2012	"One More Time"
"Our Discovery"	FrankMusik	2011	"One More Time"; "Aerodynamic"; "Technologic"
"People"	Gorillaz	2007	"Revolution 909"
"Play With Bootsy"	Bootsy Collins (featuring Kelli Ali)	2002	"Around the World"
"Pop Culture"	Madeon	2011	"Aerodynamic"; "Around the World"
"Raise It Up"	Slum Village	2001	"Extra Dry"
"Reach 4 the Sky"	Starfire (Electronic Duo)	2004	"Revolution 909"
"Recognize"	G-Side (featuring pH)	2011	"The Son of Flynn"
"Red Heat"	Skism	2012	"High Life"
"Revolution"	Marcus Intalex (featuring ST Files)	2002	"Revolution 909 (Roger Sanchez Remix)"
"Rhythm of the Night (Sexy Electro House Bitch Club Mix)"	Kid Club (featuring Sunny M.)	2010	"High Life"
"Rocket Launcher"	Sonic & Silver	2002	"Revolution 909"
"Rock It"	Sub Focus	2009	"Robot Rock"
"Run for Cover"	Mastik Soul	2009	"Technologic"
"Screamin"	Idle Warship	2009	"Oh Yeah"
"Shots One More Time"	Ace Jones	2012	"One More Time"
"Slam Dunk"	Scanty	2000	"Burnin'"
"So Much Betta"	Janet Jackson	2008	"Daftendirekt"
"Something About Us"	A.J. Crew	2009	"Something About Us"
"Something About Us"	Justt	2010	"Something About Us"

Song	Artist	Year	Daft Punk Sample/ Inspiration
"Sophisticated Bad Girl"	Colby O'Donis	2008	"Superheroes"
"Starstruck"	M-Flo (featuring Ai, Emi Hinouchi, and Rum)	2004	"Short Circuit"
"Still Skinny (Remix)"	Mind Over Matter (Aus)	2009	"Robot Rock"; "Around the World"
"Stopp & Go Original Mix"	Mirko Milano	2001	"Rollin' & Scratchin'"
"Stronger"	Kanye West	2007	"Harder, Better, Faster, Stronger"
"SummerMash '13"	DJ Earworm	2013	"Get Lucky"
"Summertime"	Wiley	2008	"Aerodynamic"
"Till It's Over"	Brianna Perry	2012	"Harder, Better, Faster, Stronger"
"Touch It"	Busta Rhymes	2005	"Technologic"
"Tuff Guy Not Tuff"	Truxton	2012	"Harder, Better, Faster, Stronger"; "One More Time"
"Tyrant"	The Bravery	2005	"Da Funk"
"Usinibore"	Just a Band	2009	"Revolution 909"
"Walkin' Around"	Dean & Ravo	2010	"Digital Love"
"War"	Boys Noize	2006	"The Prime Time of Your Life"
"Wash My World"	Laurent Wolf	2008	"Aerodynamic"
"We Up"	50 Cent (featuring Kendrick Lamar)	2013	"Something About Us"
"White Dog Problems Is What's Up"	Truxton	2012	"Short Circuit"
"Work Is Never Over"	Diplo	2007	"Harder, Better, Faster, Stronger"
"WorkItHarder"	Radium	2009	"Harder, Better, Faster, Stronger"
"Work It"	The Prototypes	2010	"Harder, Better, Faster, Stronger"
"Xyzpdqbgs"	The Left Rights	2010	"Aerodynamic"
"You Take Me (Around the World)"	JoJo	2010	"Around the World"
"Your Song"	Left Boy	2010	"Something About Us"

WHAT'S NEXT?

There aren't many musical acts that can go eight years between studio albums and remain both relevant and highly anticipated. As Daft Punk, Thomas Bangalter and Guy-Manuel de Homem-Christo find themselves among the echelons of some of their greatest influences, such as The Rolling Stones, who have managed to carve out longtime careers not only by creating innovative music, but by continuing to redefine themselves.

What's next for Daft Punk? No one really knows. In fact, it's quite possible that Bangalter and de Homem-Christo don't really know either—or if they do, they're not telling. Throughout the promotional blitz for *Random Access Memories*, the duo shied away from questions regarding new music and a new tour (there have been rumors of them possibly performing in Serbia for the first time), saying they prefer to focus on the here and now. And while they have hinted they planned out a few weeks or years down the road, they say there is no master plan. For Daft Punk, it seems their career is not only about surprising their fans, but also about surprising themselves.

After all, Daft Punk has never been the type of act to repeat itself. Bangalter and de Homem-Christo have set themselves up as the guys who can—and just might—do anything. Show up in a video game. Or a commercial. Join Kanye West on stage. Score a Disney film. Team up with Paul Williams and Pharrell Williams on the same album and have it make sense.

Even more incredible is how they've managed to stay mysterious in a digital world where there no longer seem to be any secrets, where everything happens quickly and the longevity of an artist—or a politician or a businessman—depends on constant communication with a following or fan base on multiple platforms. Daft Punk has bucked that trend. Behind shiny helmets that never reveal their faces (and change only slightly depending on their current frame of mind, much like a mood ring), they refuse to give in to the ubiquity of online promotion, eschewing the limelight for privacy, waiting until the time is right for a new endeavor (Bangalter has said it is heartening to see people respond to "artists who take their time"), and maintaining an underwhelming public profile that tantalizingly spoon-feeds select information as desired.

Perhaps after all this time, the key is that, at heart, Bangalter and de Homem-Christo still appear to be those two crazy kids making music in a bedroom. By virtually all accounts, although they may be a little more serious these days, they are still having fun and are not likely to let a little thing like a best-selling studio album change any of that. Although the duo is surprised and grateful for all the attention and kudos that *Random Access Memories* has received, Bangalter has said that Daft Punk feels no pressure to remain in the spotlight. "That's not what drives us."

What *does* drive them? It seems that Daft Punk understands something about longevity in the music business that many artists don't: the importance of taking chances, of maintaining that spark of excitement (both for themselves and for their fans), and of making music on their own terms simply because it feels right. For twenty years, Bangalter and de Homem-Christo have been upending expectations and resisting pigeonholes by doing things in their own mysterious way to the surprise and delight of their fans time and time again. And *that* is something worth waiting for—even if it takes another eight years.

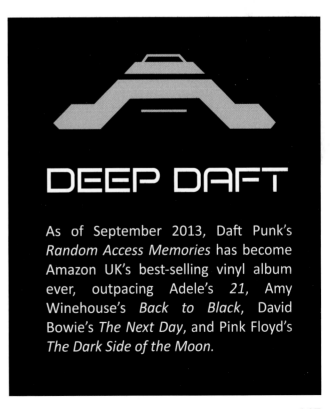

DEEP DAFT

As of September 2013, Daft Punk's *Random Access Memories* has become Amazon UK's best-selling vinyl album ever, outpacing Adele's *21*, Amy Winehouse's *Back to Black*, David Bowie's *The Next Day*, and Pink Floyd's *The Dark Side of the Moon*.

FURTHER READING/REFERENCES

Introduction

http://www.rollingstone.com/music/news/daft-punk-all-hail-our-robot-overlords-20130521
http://www.spin.com/articles/daft-punk-samples-discovery-homework-random-access-memories/?slide=16
http://www.youtube.com/watch?v=kZeRqcTO_do

The Early Years

http://www.cracked.com/funny-142-daft-punk/
http://en.wikipedia.org/wiki/Betamax
http://en.wikipedia.org/wiki/Hip_hop
http://en.wikipedia.org/wiki/The_Beach_Boys
http://en.wikipedia.org/wiki/Thomas_Bangalter
http://www.fetedelamusique.culture.fr/en/la-fete-de-la-musique/esprit-de-la-fete/
http://www.gq.com/entertainment/music/201305/daft-punk-random-access-memories-profile-gq-may-2013
http://www.guardian.co.uk/music/2013/mar/20/rocks-backpages-daft-punk
http://www.guardian.co.uk/music/2013/may/19/daft-punk-release-a-new-album
http://www.mrpopculture.com/1974
http://www.rockyhorror.com/news/pr_25thannivdvd.php
http://www.rollingstone.com/music/news/daft-punk-all-hail-our-robot-overlords-20130521
http://www.thepeoplehistory.com/1975.html
http://translate.google.com/translate?hl=en&sl=auto&tl=en&u=http://www.telerama.fr/musique/daft-punk-l-interview-fleuve,97155.php&sandbox=0&usg=ALkJrhhFIx-J9RhjouVs4ML6JNk2EXtaXg
http://translate.google.com/translate?hl=en&sl=auto&tl=en&u=http%3A%2F%2Fwww.telerama.fr%2Fmusique%2Fdaft-punk-l-interview-fleuve%2C97155.php
http://www.wild949.com/articles/chino---blog-423160/daft-punk-the-songs-that-shaped-11308504/
http://www.wired.com/thisdayintech/2011/06/0607betamax-vcr-television-recorder/
http://www.youtube.com/watch?v=kZeRqcTO_do

Early Influences

http://www.answers.com/topic/daft-punk
http://www.complex.com/music/2013/05/read-the-review-that-gave-daft-punk-their-name
http://www.daftpunk.co.uk/before-daft-punk-became-famous.php
http://www.discogs.com/artist/Darlin%27
http://en.wikipedia.org/wiki/Daft_Punk
http://entertainment.time.com/2013/05/21/robocall-a-conversation-with-daft-punk%e2%80%a8%e2%80%a8-%e2%80%a8%e2%80%a8/#ixzz2dU0EEl5c
http://www.theguardian.com/film/2007/jul/14/electronicmusic
http://www.guardian.co.uk/music/2013/mar/20/rocks-backpages-daft-punk
http://www.guardian.co.uk/music/2013/may/19/daft-punk-release-a-new-album
http://www.last.fm/music/Daft+Punk/+wiki

http://music.cbc.ca/#/blogs/2013/5/How-Daft-Punks-2006-Coachella-show-revolutionized-live-electronic-music
http://www.spin.com/articles/giorgio-moroder-daft-punk-donna-summer-interview-2013/
http://www.thedaftclub.com/forum/showthread.php/17550-quot-Review-of-Shimmies-In-Super-8-quot-Melody-Maker-May-1993
http://www.youtube.com/watch?v=eiSQcRWaxjk
http://www.youtube.com/watch?v=HHMWp9B6yJw

Origins of Electronic Dance Music

http://www.answers.com/topic/daft-punk
http://blog.oxforddictionaries.com/2012/10/the-birth-of-disco/
http://www.complex.com/music/2013/05/read-the-review-that-gave-daft-punk-their-name
http://www.daftpunk.co.uk/before-daft-punk-became-famous.php
http://www.dazeddigital.com/music/article/16291/1/cover-feature-giorgio-moroder-vs-daft-punk
http://www.deejaybooking.com/phuture303
http://www.digitaldreamdoor.com/pages/best_dance-free.html
http://www.discomusic.com/people-more/39_0_11_0_C
http://doandroidsdance.com/features/an-idiots-guide-to-edm-genres/s/house-2/
http://en.wikipedia.org/wiki/Afro-futurism
http://en.wikipedia.org/wiki/Audio_timescale-pitch_modification
http://en.wikipedia.org/wiki/Bee_Gees
http://en.wikipedia.org/wiki/Daft_Punk
http://en.wikipedia.org/wiki/Disco
http://en.wikipedia.org/wiki/DJ_Kool_Herc
http://en.wikipedia.org/wiki/Dub_music
http://en.wikipedia.org/wiki/Dubstep
http://en.wikipedia.org/wiki/Electronic_dance_music
http://en.wikipedia.org/wiki/Four_on_the_floor_%28music%29
http://en.wikipedia.org/wiki/Hi-NRG
http://en.wikipedia.org/wiki/I_Feel_Love
http://en.wikipedia.org/wiki/Jazz_funk
http://en.wikipedia.org/wiki/List_of_electronic_music_genres
http://en.wikipedia.org/wiki/Love_to_Love_You_Baby_%28song%29
http://en.wikipedia.org/wiki/Moog_synthesizer
http://en.wikipedia.org/wiki/Rapper%27s_delight
http://en.wikipedia.org/wiki/Remix
http://en.wikipedia.org/wiki/Tom_Moulton
http://en.wikipedia.org/wiki/Trance_music
http://en.wikipedia.org/wiki/Yellow_Magic_Orchestra
http://www.factmag.com/2013/05/10/a-beginners-guide-to-tom-moulton-inventor-of-the-remix-and-the-12-single/
http://grandmasterflash.com/bio/
http://www.guardian.co.uk/music/2013/mar/20/rocks-backpages-daft-punk
http://www.guardian.co.uk/music/2013/may/19/daft-punk-release-a-new-album
http://www.last.fm/music/Daft+Punk/+wiki

http://listverse.com/2011/06/01/top-10-rock-bands-that-succumbed-to-disco-fever/
http://moogfoundation.org/about/humble-visionary/bob-moog-timeline/
http://music.cbc.ca/#/blogs/2013/5/How-Daft-Punks-2006-Coachella-show-revolutionized-live-electronic-music
http://www.newsday.com/entertainment/music/dj-kool-herc-still-in-the-groove-1.4655366
http://www.oldschoolhiphop.com/artists/deejays/kooldjherc.htm
http://openvault.wgbh.org/catalog/9fc448-interview-with-malcolm-cecil-and-robert-margouleff-part-1-of-2
http://www.pbs.org/wgbh/pages/frontline/shows/music/inside/cron.html
http://pitchfork.com/news/51874-giorgio-moroder-hot-chip-frankie-knuckles-set-for-donna-summer-remix-album/http://www.soundonsound.com/sos/mar98/articles/giorgio.html
http://www.residentadvisor.net/dj/grandflash/biography
http://searchcio-midmarket.techtarget.com/definition/vocoder
http://www.songfacts.com/detail.php?id=1077
http://www.soundonsound.com/sos/oct09/articles/classictracks_1009.htm
http://www.spin.com/articles/giorgio-moroder-daft-punk-donna-summer-interview-2013/
http://www.telegraph.co.uk/culture/music/3654400/How-the-Nazis-gave-us-disco.html
http://www.theguardian.com/news/2005/may/16/guardianobituaries.france
http://www.theguardian.com/music/2011/sep/29/skrillex-dubstep-interview
http://www.wired.com/wired/archive/2.07/techno_pr.html
http://www.youtube.com/watch?v=eYDvxo-M0OQ
http://www.youtube.com/watch?v=ybufC_3KJwk
Peter Shapiro, ed., *Modulations: A History of Electronic Music: Throbbing Words on Sound* (Caipirinha), 2000.

Forming the Duo

http://www.brooklynvegan.com/archives/2010/10/daft_punk_playe.html
http://www.daftpunk-anthology.com/dpa/daft-story/daft-punk
http://en.wikipedia.org/wiki/Phasing_%28music%29
http://en.wikipedia.org/wiki/Thomas_Bangalter
http://www.gq.com/entertainment/music/201305/daft-punk-random-access-memories-profile-gq-may-2013
http://www.npr.org/2013/05/16/184499357/daft-punk-on-the-soul-that-a-musician-can-bring
http://www.nytimes.com/2007/07/01/arts/music/01herm.html?pagewanted=print&_r=0
http://pitchfork.com/features/staff-lists/7853-the-top-200-tracks-of-the-1990s-20-01/
http://www.rollingstone.com/music/news/ed-banger-records-turns-10-20130802
http://www.thevinyldistrict.com/storefront/2013/07/screamadelica-why-primal-screams-1991-opus-was-the-most-important-album-of-the-year/
http://translate.google.com/translate?hl=en&sl=auto&tl=en&u=http%3A%2F%2Fwww.telerama.fr%2Fmusique%2Fdaft-punk-l-interview-fleuve%2C97155.php
http://usatoday30.usatoday.com/news/world/2008-11-06-3567088143_x.htm
http://www.villagevoice.com/2007-03-20/music/friends-forever/
http://www.youtube.com/watch?v=kZeRqcTO_do

Homework

http://www.azlyrics.com/lyrics/daftpunk/teachers.html
http://daftpunk.wikia.com/wiki/Daftendirekt
http://daftpunk.wikia.com/wiki/Revolution_909
http://daftpunk.wikia.com/wiki/WDPK_83.7_Fm
http://dancemusic.about.com/cs/interviews/a/IntDaftPunkDave_3.htm
http://en.wikipedia.org/wiki/Tony_Maxwell
http://www.gq.com/entertainment/music/201305/daft-punk-random-access-memories-profile-gq-may-2013
http://www.guardian.co.uk/music/2013/may/19/daft-punk-release-a-new-album
http://music.cbc.ca/#/blogs/2013/6/Daft-Punk-unmasked-a-timeline-of-the-duos-real-faces
http://pitchfork.com/features/staff-lists/7853-the-top-200-tracks-of-the-1990s-20-01/
http://www.rollingstone.com/music/artists/daft-punk/albumguide
http://www.theatlantic.com/entertainment/archive/2013/05/daft-punks-i-random-access-memories-i-is-a-lovely-sounding-retirement-record/275941/
http://www.thedaftclub.com/forum/showthread.php/10993-Interesting-findings-in-the-liner-notes-of-Homework
http://www.thedaftclub.com/forum/showthread.php/16717-The-Meaning-Of-Daftendirekt
http://theinterrobang.com/2012/03/the-5-spike-jonze-music-videos/
http://www.vibe.com/article/exclusive-nile-rodgers-shooting-videos-daft-punk-collaborating-david-guetta-avicii
http://www.waxpoetics.com/features/articles/quantum-leap/2
http://web.archive.org/web/20110606041352/http://www.montrealmirror.com/ARCHIVES/1997/040397/cover.html
http://www.wild949.com/articles/chino---blog-423160/daft-punk-the-songs-that-shaped-11308504/

D.A.F.T: A Story About Dogs, Androids, Firemen and Tomatoes

http://en.wikipedia.org/wiki/D.A.F.T.:_A_Story_About_Dogs,_Androids,_Firemen_and_Tomatoes
http://www.thedaftclub.com/films/daft-a-story-about-dogs-androids-firemen-and-tomatoes/
http://www.youtube.com/watch?v=uURB-vo9rZ4&list=PL1BB506AD3D6ACC13

Alive 1997

http://www.armandvanhelden.com/
http://www.billboard.com/articles/news/80637/garth-notches-best-selling-live-album-ever
http://en.wikipedia.org/wiki/500_Greatest_Albums_of_All_Time
http://en.wikipedia.org/wiki/Alive_1997
http://en.wikipedia.org/wiki/Daft_Club
http://en.wikipedia.org/wiki/Live_album
http://lescharts.com/showitem.asp?interpret=Daft+Punk&titel=Alive+1997&cat=a
http://www.thedaftclub.com/tour-dates/daftendirektour-1997/
http://theworldisdaft.wordpress.com/2010/01/31/daft-punk-live-the-red-box-dublin-oct-1997-missing-bootleg/

Going Solo

http://www.allmusic.com/album/waves-vol-2-mw0000027202
http://www.daftpunk-anthology.com/music/labels/scratche
http://www.djbroadcast.net/features/featureitem_id=27/Blueprint_Labels_Roul_Records.html
http://www.djtimes.com/original/djmag/may01/daft.htm
http://en.wikipedia.org/wiki/Guy-Manuel_de_Homem-Christo
http://en.wikipedia.org/wiki/Roul%C3%A9
http://en.wikipedia.org/wiki/Thomas_Bangalter
http://www.inthemix.com/news/54064/Hey_Daft_Punk_fans_Thomas_Bangalters_1995_EP_gets_a_reissue
http://thequietus.com/articles/05097-gaspar-no-interview-enter-the-void-soundtrack-daft-punk
http://web.archive.org/web/20080503064751/http://remixmag.com/mag/remix_robopop/

Discovery

http://anthemmagazine.com/the-work-of-art-is-controlling-you/
http://www.djtimes.com/original/djmag/may01/daft.htm
http://en.wikipedia.org/wiki/Discovery_%28Daft_Punk_album%29
http://en.wikipedia.org/wiki/One_More_Time_%28Daft_Punk_song%29
http://huntnewsnu.com/2013/07/column-daft-punks-reign-of-techno/
http://www.independent.co.uk/news/obituaries/romanthony-dj-and-producer-who-sang-for-daft-punk-8744271.html
http://www.mixmag.net/words/news/what-is-the-greatest-dance-track-of-all-time
http://mixonline.com/mag/audio_daft_punk/
http://www.rollingstone.com/music/news/one-more-time-singer-romanthony-dead-at-45-20130519
http://www.thedaftclub.com/forum/showthread.php/16852-Daft-Punk-interview-in-quot-The-Evolution-of-Electronic-Dance-Music-quot/page2
http://web.archive.org/web/20080503064751/http://remixmag.com/mag/remix_robopop/
http://www.youtube.com/watch?v=kZeRqcTO_do
http://www.youtube.com/watch?v=kM4neTsgTZo

Interstella 5555: The 5tory of the 5ecret 5tar 5ystem

http://www.dazeddigital.com/music/article/594/1/daft-punks-electroma
http://en.wikipedia.org/wiki/Interstella_5555:_The_5tory_of_the_5ecret_5tar_5ystem
http://en.wikipedia.org/wiki/Leiji_Matsumoto
http://www.thefader.com/2013/06/28/daft-punk-the-creators/

Daft Club

http://www.djtimes.com/original/djmag/may01/daft.htm
http://en.wikipedia.org/wiki/Daft_Club

Human After All

http://www.allmusic.com/album/release/human-after-all-mr0001565064
http://www.billboard.com/articles/news/59839/billboard-bits-daft-punk-van-morrison-elf-power
http://daftpunk.wikia.com/wiki/Human_After_All_%28album%29

http://daftpunk.wikia.com/wiki/Human_After_All:_Remixes
http://en.wikipedia.org/wiki/Human_After_All
http://entertainment.time.com/2013/05/21/robocall-a-conversation-with-daft-punk%E2%80%A8%E2%80%A8-%E2%80%A8%E2%80%A8/
http://www.gq.com/entertainment/music/201305/daft-punk-random-access-memories-profile-gq-may-2013
http://www.mixmag.net/events/holidays/daft-punk
http://www.papermag.com/2013/05/daft_punk_and_the_rise_of_the.php
http://prettymuchamazing.com/mp3/daft-punk-remix-album-to-be-released-may-20
http://translate.google.com/translate?hl=en&sl=auto&tl=en&u=http%3A%2F%2Fwww.telerama.fr%2Fmusique%2Fdaft-punk-l-interview-fleuve%2C97155.php

Daft Punk's Electroma

http://www.clashmusic.com/feature/electroma
http://closetonefilms.wordpress.com/tag/electroma/
http://www.dazeddigital.com/music/article/3496/1/dazed-digital-exclusive-daft-arts-video
http://en.wikipedia.org/wiki/Daft_Punk%27s_Electroma
http://en.wikipedia.org/wiki/Tony_Gardner_%28designer%29
http://www.gq.com/entertainment/music/201305/daft-punk-random-access-memories-profile-gq-may-2013
http://www.heraldsun.com.au/entertainment/movies/midnight-feast-of-sights-and-sound/story-e6frf9h6-1111113611533
http://www.theage.com.au/news/film/from-the-desert-the-robots-come/2007/06/07/1181089191457.html
http://www.thedaftclub.com/forum/showthread.php/13893-Independence-CA-5-Years-After-Electroma
http://www.theguardian.com/film/2007/jul/14/electronicmusic
http://variety.com/2006/film/reviews/daft-punk-s-electroma-1200516026/

Musique, Vol. 1 1993–2005

http://www.billboard.com/artist/300085/Daft+Punk/chart?f=322
http://daftpunk.wikia.com/wiki/Robot_Rock
http://en.wikipedia.org/wiki/Musique_Vol._1_1993%E2%80%932005

Alive 2006/2007

http://archives.lasvegascitylife.com/articles/2007/10/25/news/cover/iq_17439539.prt
http://www.billboard.com/articles/news/59839/billboard-bits-daft-punk-van-morrison-elf-power
http://en.wikipedia.org/wiki/Alive_2006/2007
http://en.wikipedia.org/wiki/Alive_2007
http://en.wikipedia.org/wiki/Technologic
http://www.gq.com/entertainment/music/201305/daft-punk-random-access-memories-profile-gq-may-2013
http://www.laweekly.com/2007-10-25/music/buy-it-use-it-break-it-fix-it/
http://music.cbc.ca/#/blogs/2013/5/How-Daft-Punks-2006-Coachella-show-revolutionized-live-electronic-music

http://pitchfork.com/reviews/albums/10925-alive-2007/
http://www.rollingstone.com/music/news/daft-punk-all-hail-our-robot-overlords-20130521
http://vimeo.com/32016510

Alive 2007

http://www.billboard.com/articles/news/1049888/exclusive-live-album-to-chronicle-daft-punk-tour
http://en.wikipedia.org/wiki/Alive_2007
http://en.wikipedia.org/wiki/Harder,_Better,_Faster,_Stronger
http://en.wikipedia.org/wiki/Palais_Omnisports_de_Paris-Bercy
http://imvdb.com/video/the-stills/lola-stars-and-stripes
http://www.mvdbase.com/tech.php?id=2581
http://www.youtube.com/watch?v=AH9uneXSdFM

TRON: Legacy

http://culturemob.com/soundtrack-review-daft-punks-classical-meets-cyberpunk-approach-to-tron-legacy
http://www.dazeddigital.com/music/article/9170/1/daft-punk-encore
https://www.disneyconsumerproducts.com/Home/display.jsp?contentId=dcp_home_pressroom_pressreleases_dcp_home_pr_us_tron_daft_age=en&preview=false&imageShow=0&pressRoom=US&translationOf=null%C2%AEion=0&ccPK=dcp_home_pressroom_press_room_all_US
http://en.wikipedia.org/wiki/Tron:_Legacy
http://en.wikipedia.org/wiki/Tron:_Legacy_%28soundtrack%29
http://www.guardian.co.uk/music/2013/may/19/daft-punk-release-a-new-album
http://www.imdb.com/media/rm3242570752/nm2468967
http://www.kcrw.com/music/programs/mb/mb101129tron_legacy_soundtra
http://moviesblog.mtv.com/2009/07/23/tron-legacy-panel-report-fresh-from-san-diego-comic-con
http://somethingelsereviews.com/2013/07/20/on-second-thought-daft-punk-tron-legacy-soundtrack-2010/
http://translate.google.com/translate?hl=en&sl=auto&tl=en&u=http%3A%2F%2Fwww.telerama.fr%2Fmusique%2Fdaft-punk-l-interview-fleuve%2C97155.php
http://tron.wikia.com/wiki/MediCom_Toy
http://web.archive.org/web/20101104035555/http://www.waltdisneystudiosawards.com/tronlegacy/music.php
http://www.youtube.com/watch?v=WKi5q2ZpiRI

Pop Culture Icons

http://deadspin.com/mike-doc-emricks-passing-synonyms-a-daft-punk-mashu-514047086
http://doandroidsdance.com/features/the-10-best-daft-punk-appearances-in-mainstream-media/s/louis-vuitton-springsummer-2008-show-2/
http://en.wikipedia.org/wiki/Daft_Punk
http://en.wikipedia.org/wiki/DJ_Hero
http://en.wikipedia.org/wiki/Technologic
http://www.ign.com/articles/2009/10/23/daft-punk-worst-to-best

http://www.imdb.com/title/tt1006987/quotes
http://www.myvirtualpaper.com/doc/WhiteWall/WW-SU09-COMB/2009052001/#92
http://www.nintendo-insider.com/2013/09/06/daft-punks-get-lucky-joins-just-dance-2014-tracklist/
http://www.nydailynews.com/life-style/fashion/hedi-slimane-designs-stage-gear-daft-punk-article-1.1316935
http://noisey.vice.com/blog/a-history-of-daft-punk-appearing-in-commercials-for-things-1
http://www.pastemagazine.com/articles/2010/06/adidas-star-wars-world-cup-commercial.html
http://pitchfork.com/news/39042-daft-punk-do-star-wars-for-adidas/
http://pitchfork.com/news/48891-watch-daft-punk-on-the-simpsons-sort-of/
http://popschau.wordpress.com/2013/06/23/the-brand-daft-punk-all-commercials-from-the-last-12-years/
http://www.psfk.com/2013/03/yves-saint-laurent-rebranding.html
http://www.theocmusic.co.uk/php/Season_2/episode19_season2_theoc.php

The Helmets and Outfits

"A Visual History of Daft Punk's Helmets," elektro, Summer 2013, 30.
http://en.wikipedia.org/wiki/Hedi_Slimane
http://enlighted.com/pages/daftpunk2007.shtml
http://exclaim.ca/News/daft_punk_unveil_new_outfits_share_album_details_with_new_trailer_unveil_kanye_west_team-up
http://www.gq.com/entertainment/music/201305/daft-punk-random-access-memories-profile-gq-may-2013
http://www.gq.com/style/wear-it-now/200511/dior-clothing-designer-hedi-silmane?currentPage=2
http://www.guardian.co.uk/music/2013/mar/20/rocks-backpages-daft-punk
http://www.guardian.co.uk/music/2013/may/19/daft-punk-release-a-new-album
http://www.last.fm/music/Daft+Punk/+wiki
http://www.laweekly.com/2007-10-25/music/buy-it-use-it-break-it-fix-it/
http://www.mixmag.net/events/holidays/daft-punk
http://motherboard.vice.com/blog/random-access-criticism
http://music.cbc.ca/#/blogs/2013/6/Daft-Punk-unmasked-a-timeline-of-the-duos-real-faces
http://online.wsj.com/article/SB10001424127887324031404578481680129191190.html
http://www.phantomoftheparadise.ca/why2.html
http://pitchfork.com/reviews/albums/10925-alive-2007/
http://www.rollingstone.com/music/news/daft-punk-all-hail-our-robot-overlords-20130521
http://www.spin.com/articles/giorgio-moroder-daft-punk-donna-summer-interview-2013/
http://www.thedaftclub.com/features/a-visual-history-of-daft-punks-helmets/
http://www.theguardian.com/fashion/fashion-blog/2013/may/16/daft-punk-helmet-robot-style-evolution
http://translate.google.com/translate?hl=en&sl=auto&tl=en&u=http%3A%2F%2Fwww.telerama.fr%2Fmusique%2Fdaft-punk-l-interview-fleuve%2C97155.php
http://www.vogue.com/magazine/article/what-to-wear-where-all-ages-show-karlie-kloss-and-daft-punk/#1
http://www.youtube.com/watch?v=H0TBZeCgL0E

Random Access Memories: The Buildup

http://www.abc.net.au/news/2013-04-13/wee-waa-braces-for-daft-punk-duo/4625344

http://articles.latimes.com/2013/apr/13/entertainment/la-et-ms-coachella-2013-longing-for-daft-punk-20130413

http://www.billboard.com/articles/news/1556730/daft-punk-to-launch-new-album-at-australian-agricultural-fest

http://www.billboard.com/biz/articles/news/branding/1557425/daft-punk-tease-new-album-at-coachella-during-saturday-night-live

http://brand-e.biz/daft-punk-get-lucky-ad-tweets-trigger-music-sales_29638.html

http://www.businessweek.com/articles/2013-06-27/daft-punks-get-lucky-how-to-build-the-song-of-the-summer

http://consequenceofsound.net/2013/04/daft-punk-launch-new-video-series-watch-giorgio-moroder-discuss-their-new-album/

http://consequenceofsound.net/2013/04/daft-punk-tease-new-music-at-coachella-featuring-julian-casablancas-and-panda-bear/

http://www.dancingastronaut.com/2013/01/daft-punk-signs-with-sony-fourth-album-to-be-released-this-spring/

http://en.wikipedia.org/wiki/Random_Access_Memories

http://en.wikipedia.org/wiki/Random_Access_Memories#Promotion

http://entertainment.time.com/2013/05/21/robocall-a-conversation-with-daft-punk%E2%80%A8%E2%80%A8-%E2%80%A8%E2%80%A8/

http://www.gq.com/entertainment/music/201305/daft-punk-random-access-memories-profile-gq-may-2013

http://www.hollywoodreporter.com/earshot/daft-punk-signs-columbia-records-415666

http://www.huffingtonpost.com/2013/04/17/daft-punk-get-lucky-leaked-full-song-pharrell-williams_n_3102455.html

http://www.inthemix.com/news/54922/Sonys_site_lists_Daft_Punk_for_Coachella

http://www.inthemix.com/news/55021/Daft_Punks_Wee_Waa_album_launch_Everything_you_need_to_know

http://kroq.cbslocal.com/2013/01/28/will-daft-punk-join-phoenix-onstage-at-coachella-2013-its-happened-before/

http://www.mixmag.net/words/news/its-as-good-as-anything-ive-ever-done-nile-rodgers-talks-working-with-daft-punk

http://www.mixmag.net/words/news/nile-rodgers-reckons-new-daft-punk-material-will-be-out-in-2013

http://www.mtv.com/news/articles/1705910/daft-punk-get-lucky-release.jhtml

http://www.nilerodgers.com/blogs/planet-c-in-english/2588-2013-won-t-be-boring

http://pitchfork.com/news/49696-daft-punk-confirm-signing-to-columbia/

http://pitchfork.com/news/49993-sony-registers-13-new-daft-punk-songs/

http://www.rollingstone.com/music/news/listen-to-daft-punks-new-album-random-access-memories-20130513

http://www.spin.com/articles/daft-punk-random-access-memories-track-list-vine

http://stoneyroads.com/daft-punk-album-solidifies-with-sony-registering-new-tracks/

http://www.thecourier.net.au/news-feed/item/1311-grammy-award-winning-daft-punk-to-launch-album-here

http://www.thedaftclub.com/2013/01/27/daft-punk-signs-with-colombia-records-album-due-in-spring/

http://www.theguardian.com/music/2013/jan/28/daft-punk-to-release-album

http://www.thelmagazine.com/TheMeasure/archives/2013/04/15/this-daft-punk-hype-blitz-is-silly-confusing-and-super-effective

http://translate.google.com/translate?hl=en&sl=auto&tl=en&u=http%3A%2F%2Fwww.telerama.fr%2Fmusique%2Fdaft-punk-l-interview-fleuve%2C97155.php

http://www.wired.com/underwire/2013/05/daft-punk-wee-waa-premiere/

http://www.youtube.com/watch?v=Rr12u1tk_rM

The New Sound

http://www.billboard.com/articles/columns/code/1560708/daft-punk-on-edm-producers-theyre-missing-the-tools

http://blogs.lowellsun.com/sweetpetes/2013/05/22/review-daft-punk-takes-memories-into-future/?doing_wp_cron=1374011735.3549470901489257812500

http://www.daftpunk-anthology.com/random-access-memories-return-decrypted-7777

http://www.daftpunk-anthology.com/second-track-the-game-of-love-9824

http://www.dazeddigital.com/music/article/16147/1/nile-rodgerss-five-favourite-daft-punk-records

http://en.wikipedia.org/wiki/Random_Access_Memories

http://www.gigwise.com/news/81136/william-compares-daft-punk-single-to-michael-jacksons-thriller

http://www.gq.com/entertainment/music/201305/daft-punk-random-access-memories-profile-gq-may-2013

http://hifimagazine.net/blog/?p=7775#

http://www.mtv.com/news/articles/1708517/daft-punk-pharrell-williams-get-lucky.jhtml

http://www.newyorker.com/arts/critics/musical/2013/05/27/130527crmu_music_frerejones

http://www.npr.org/blogs/therecord/2013/05/14/183939750/robots-in-ecstasy-daft-punks-memories-embraces-the-pleasure-principle

http://obsession.nouvelobs.com/musique/20130426.OBS7299/daft-punk-nous-avons-tente-une-aventure-humaine.html

http://pitchfork.com/reviews/albums/18028-daft-punk-random-access-memories/

http://popdust.com/2013/05/21/daft-punks-random-access-memories-reviewed-motherboard/

http://productionadvice.co.uk/daft-punk-mastering/

http://www.rollingstone.com/music/news/daft-punk-all-hail-our-robot-overlords-20130521

http://www.rollingstone.com/music/news/exclusive-daft-punk-reveal-secrets-of-new-album-20130413

http://www.spin.com/articles/daft-punk-get-lucky-pharrell-leak-real-fake/

http://www.spin.com/reviews/daft-punk-random-access-memories-columbia/

http://www.theatlantic.com/entertainment/archive/2013/05/daft-punks-i-random-access-memories-i-is-a-lovely-sounding-retirement-record/275941/

http://translate.google.com/translate?hl=en&sl=auto&tl=en&u=http%3A%2F%2Fobsession.nouvelobs.com%2Fmusique%2F20130418.OBS6224%2Frandom-access-memories-par-daft-punk.html

Random Access Memories: The Studios

http://articles.latimes.com/2011/may/29/entertainment/la-ca-capitolrecords-20110529

www.billboard.com/articles/columns/code/1560708/daft-punk-on-edm-producers-theyre-missing-the-tools

http://www.billboard.com/articles/columns/code/1561328/daft-punk-how-the-pioneering-dance-duo-conjured-random-access-memories

http://www.billboard.com/articles/review/1554419/the-strokes-comedown-machine-track-by-track-review

http://www.capitolstudios.com/studios/

http://consequenceofsound.net/2013/07/album-review-daftside-random-access-memories-memories-2/

http://en.wikipedia.org/wiki/Capitol_Studios

http://en.wikipedia.org/wiki/Charlie_Chaplin_Studios

http://en.wikipedia.org/wiki/Comedown_Machine

http://en.wikipedia.org/wiki/Conway_Recording_Studios

http://en.wikipedia.org/wiki/Electric_Lady_Studios

http://en.wikipedia.org/wiki/Minetta_Creek

http://en.wikipedia.org/wiki/Positif_%28album%29

http://en.wikipedia.org/wiki/Random_Access_Memories

http://www.guitarworld.com/interview-bassist-nathan-east-discusses-fourplays-new-album-and-his-days-eric-clapton

http://gvshp.org/blog/2013/08/26/happy-birthday-electric-lady-studios/

http://www.hensonrecording.com/history.html

http://www.historyofrecording.com/electric_lady_studios.html

http://jonathangrand.com/conwayrecording.com/history/

http://nathaneast.com/biography/

http://www.nytimes.com/2010/08/26/arts/music/26hendrix.html?_r=0

https://soundbetter.com/profiles/538-gang-studio

http://www.studioexpresso.com/Spotlight%20Archive/Spotlight%20Conway.htm

http://thetalkhouse.com/reviews/view/dean-wareham-daft-punk

http://translate.google.com/translate?hl=en&sl=auto&tl=en&u=http%3A%2F%2Fwww.telerama.fr%2Fmusique%2Fdaft-punk-l-interview-fleuve%2C97155.php

http://translate.google.com/translate?hl=en&sl=fr&u=http://fr.wikipedia.org/wiki/Claude_Puterflam&prev=/search%3Fq%3DClaude%2BPuterflam%2Bwiki%26biw%3D1600%26bih%3D701

http://www.wsdg.com/portfolio.asp?id=ELECTRICLADY http://www.youtube.com/watch?v=eiTO30HrThw

http://www.youtube.com/watch?v=yf2buOP_4Vo

The Collaborators: Pharrell Williams

http://www.artistdirect.com/nad/news/article/0,,7321764,00.html

http://www.billboard.com/articles/columns/the-hook/1562309/pharrell-williams-joins-rihannas-styled-to-rock-competition-series

http://www.billboard.com/articles/news/1566896/the-summer-song-of-2013-will-daft-punk-get-lucky

http://en.wikipedia.org/wiki/Blurred_Lines

http://en.wikipedia.org/wiki/Get_Lucky_%28Daft_Punk_song%29

http://en.wikipedia.org/wiki/Phoenix_%28mythology%29

http://www.forbes.com/sites/zackomalleygreenburg/2012/11/16/pharrell-williams-next-gig-internet-talk-show-host/

http://www.gigwise.com/news/81182/pharrell-to-make-kylie-no-doubt-jay-z-and-beyonce-cooler

http://www.gq.com/entertainment/music/201305/daft-punk-random-access-memories-profile-gq-may-2013

http://www.hollywoodreporter.com/live-feed/rihannas-styled-rock-competition-series-559364

http://www.instyle.com/instyle/package/general/photos/0,,20207686_20185882_20439904,00.html#20439904

http://www.mtv.com/news/articles/1449404/pharrell-williams-rb-revolt.jhtml

http://n-e-r-d.com/about/

http://www.mtv.com/news/articles/1709697/pharrell-despicable-me-2-soundtrack.jhtml

http://www.newyorker.com/online/blogs/sashafrerejones/2013/06/daft-punk-random-access-memories-leaked-reviews.html

http://www.nytimes.com/2013/07/21/arts/music/robin-thicke-a-romantic-has-a-naughty-hit.html?pagewanted=all

http://rock.rapgenius.com/Daft-punk-get-lucky-lyrics#note-1685964

http://www.rollingstone.com/music/videos/pharrell-daft-punk-not-bound-by-time-and-space-20130415

http://spinoff.comicbookresources.com/2013/07/03/pharrell-williams-explores-the-happier-side-of-things-for-despicable-me-2/

http://www.vulture.com/2013/06/pharrell-williams-interview.html

https://www.youtube.com/watch?v=6QVtHogFrI0

http://www.youtube.com/watch?v=A6PEboTpcfI

http://www.youtube.com/watch?v=SkCn-iWLiSE

The Collaborators: Paul Williams

http://artsbeat.blogs.nytimes.com/2012/06/02/the-good-guys-and-bad-guys-that-ive-been-paul-williams-on-paul-williams-still-alive/

http://www.ascap.com/about/board-intro.aspx

http://en.wikipedia.org/wiki/Paul_Williams_%28songwriter%29

http://en.wikipedia.org/wiki/Phantom_of_the_Paradise

http://en.wikipedia.org/wiki/Random_Access_Memories

http://www.hensonrecording.com/

http://www.nme.com/news/nme/70731

http://www.phantomoftheparadise.ca/why2.html

http://pitchfork.com/features/cover-story/9131-daft-punk/

http://www.spin.com/articles/daft-punk-random-access-memories-track-by-track-preview/

https://www.youtube.com/watch?v=2n5qVJEg3qA

https://www.youtube.com/watch?v=C683ACADxkw

The Collaborators: Nile Rodgers

http://www.belfasttelegraph.co.uk/entertainment/music/from-chic-to-the-big-c-how-disco-legend-nile-rodgers-got-lucky-29449763.html

http://www.dazeddigital.com/music/article/16147/1/nile-rodgerss-five-favourite-daft-punk-records

http://en.wikipedia.org/wiki/Get_Lucky_%28Daft_Punk_song%29

http://www.fasterlouder.com.au/features/31745/Chic

http://www.heraldscotland.com/arts-ents/music/im-proud-our-music-has-an-evergreen-quality-to-it-but-it-does-feel-dated-to-me-because-i-dont-remember-making-it

http://www.independent.ie/entertainment/music/feeling-lucky-29434696.html
http://metro.co.uk/2013/07/26/nile-rodgers-i-had-sex-with-a-celebrity-at-studio-54-but-i-wont-say-any-names-3898714/?ITO=news-sitemap
http://www.nilerodgers.com/about/biography
http://nilerodgers.com/blogs/planet-c-in-english/2717-bad-news-travels-fast
http://www.rollingstone.com/music/videos/daft-punk-and-nile-rodgers-will-collaborate-again-20130710
http://www.youtube.com/watch?v=da_Yp9BOCaI

The Collaborators: Giorgio Moroder

http://www.dazeddigital.com/music/article/16291/1/cover-feature-giorgio-moroder-vs-daft-punk
http://www.dazeddigital.com/music/article/16141/1/daft-punk-vs-giorgio-moroder
http://en.wikipedia.org/wiki/Giorgio_Moroder
http://news.yahoo.com/blogs/newsmakers/synth-disco-legend-giorgio-moroder-daft-punk-collaboration-135423986.html
http://noisey.vice.com/blog/giorgio-moroder-discusses-collaborating-on-daft-punks-new-album-random-access-memories
http://www.rollingstone.com/music/news/giorgio-moroder-sits-down-for-lengthy-fireside-chat-plays-influential-tracks-20130723
http://www.soundonsound.com/sos/mar98/articles/giorgio.html
http://www.spin.com/articles/giorgio-moroder-daft-punk-donna-summer-interview-2013/
http://www.synthtopia.com/content/2012/04/26/happy-birthday-giorgio-moroder/#more-40021

The Collaborators: Panda Bear

http://animalcollective.org/biography
http://www.billboard.com/articles/review/1561414/daft-punk-random-access-memories-track-by-track-review
http://en.wikipedia.org/wiki/Animal_Collective
http://en.wikipedia.org/wiki/Around_the_World_%28Daft_Punk_song%29
http://en.wikipedia.org/wiki/Panda_Bear_%28musician%29
http://en.wikipedia.org/wiki/Random_Access_Memories
http://www.last.fm/music/Animal+Collective
http://motherboard.vice.com/read/animal-collective-on-daft-punk-no-masks
http://www.nme.com/news/daft-punk/69932
http://pitchfork.com/reviews/albums/18028-daft-punk-random-access-memories/
http://prettymuchamazing.com/music/recd/daft-punk-panda-bear-doing-it-right
http://www.slate.com/blogs/browbeat/2013/05/28/daft_punk_get_lucky_ultimate_dance_compilation_watch_movie_characters_dance.html
http://www.spin.com/articles/daft-punk-get-lucky-condom-durex/
http://thecreatorsproject.vice.com/about
http://thecreatorsproject.vice.com/blog/animal-collective-daft-punk-random-access-memories the-collaborators-noah-lennox
http://www.youtube.com/watch?v=Q8jmBbG4T6c

The Collaborators: Julian Casablancas

http://www.allmusic.com/artist/julian-casablancas-mn0000337135
http://en.wikipedia.org/wiki/Julian_Casablancas
http://en.wikipedia.org/wiki/Random_Access_Memories
http://www.news.com.au/entertainment/music/daft-punk-find-the-human-touch/story-fn93z1ud-1226638326325
http://www.nme.com/news/the-strokes/36666
http://www.spin.com/articles/daft-punk-random-access-memories-track-by-track-preview/
http://www.spin.com/articles/spin-interview-julian-casablancas/
http://thestrokesnews.com/nme-discusses-daft-punks-instant-crush-which-features-julian-casablancas/

The Collaborators: Todd Edwards

http://www.duttyartz.com/blog/nj-garage-todd-edwards/
http://en.wikipedia.org/wiki/Todd_Edwards
http://www.factmag.com/2013/05/13/todd-edwards-confirms-bbc-essential-mix-promises-glut-of-exclusive-material/
http://hifimagazine.net/blog/?p=7775#
http://www.redbullmusicacademy.com/lectures/todd-edwards
http://www.stylusmagazine.com/articles/weekly_article/todd-edwards-the-stylus-interview.htm
http://tmagazine.blogs.nytimes.com/2013/05/14/q-a-daft-punks-secret-weapon-producer-todd-edwards/?_r=0
http://www.youtube.com/watch?v=yf2bu0P_4Vo

The Collaborators: Chilly Gonzales

http://chillygonzales.com/records/le-guinness-world-record-friends-of-mine/
http://en.wikipedia.org/wiki/Gonzales_%28musician%29
http://exclaim.ca/News/chilly_gonzales_announces_first-ever_all-orchestral_rap_album_live_show
http://www.theglobeandmail.com/arts/summer-entertainment/the-fall-and-rise-of-chilly-gonzales/article12414638/
http://m.npr.org/news/NPR+Music+Mobile/159925301
http://pitchfork.com/news/36532-gonzales-challenges-andrew-wk-to-a-piano-battle-in-nyc-and-he-accepts/
http://www.playgroundmag.net/music/music-magazine-articles/music-interviews/gonzales-i-dont-think-music-is-a-right-i-believe-in-a-way-that-the-free-market-does-work-when-it-comes-to-it
http://www.sheenabeaston.com/sheena-beaston/2010/02/peaches-christ-superstar-featuring-chilly-gonzales-live-performance-details.html
http://www.stereogum.com/1222632/feistdrake-collaborator-chilly-gonzales-on-the-surprise-success-of-his-solo-piano-albums-and-turning-classical-into-pop/interview/
http://www.theguardian.com/music/2009/may/20/gonzales-longest-solo-concert
http://www.theguardian.com/music/2012/oct/21/chilly-gonzales-bbc-symphony-orchestra-review
http://www.tumblr.com/tagged/chilly-gonzales?before=1316005584
http://www.youtube.com/watch?v=btfbIVGES1I
http://www.youtube.com/watch?v=Kc3I0Ent9Zg
http://www.youtube.com/watch?v=lI9F9p5LFWw

The Collaborators: DJ Falcon

http://www.discogs.com/artist/Together+%282%29
http://en.wikipedia.org/wiki/DJ_Falcon
http://en.wikipedia.org/wiki/Random_Access_Memories
http://www.factmag.com/2013/05/01/stream-an-early-version-of-contact-the-dj-falcon-featuring-closer-from-daft-punks-random-access-memories/
http://www.factmag.com/2013/05/13/daft-punk-collaborator-dj-falcon-working-on-original-material-again-plans-ep-and-potential-album/
http://www.fakeartists.com/?portfolio=dj-falcon
http://pitchfork.com/news/50559-listen-to-an-early-version-of-daft-punks-random-access-memories-track-contact-with-dj-falcon/
http://pitchfork.com/reviews/albums/18028-daft-punk-random-access-memories/
http://popdust.com/2013/05/21/daft-punks-random-access-memories-reviewed-contact/
http://www.rollingstone.com/music/videos/paul-williams-dj-falcon-describe-working-with-daft-punk-20130510
http://thecreatorsproject.vice.com/blog/meet-the-collaborators-behind-daft-punks-irandom-access-memoriesi-episode-7---dj-falcon
http://www.youtube.com/watch?v=gca9hrmVapE

The Collaborators: John "JR" Robinson and Omar Hakim

Bob McKinley, "Single Strokes," DRUM!, August 2013, 20.
http://www.billboard.com/articles/columns/code/1561328/daft-punk-how-the-pioneering-dance-duo-conjured-random-access-memories
http://www.classicfm.com/composers/zimmer/news/hans-zimmer-drum-percussion-man-steel-sessions/
http://en.wikipedia.org/wiki/John_Robinson_%28drummer%29
http://en.wikipedia.org/wiki/Omar_Hakim
http://en.wikipedia.org/wiki/Random_Access_Memories
http://en.wikipedia.org/wiki/Weather_Report
http://www.johnjrrobinson.com/#
http://www.omarhakim.com/
http://orisonmusic.blogspot.com/2009/06/quinn-is-recording-artist-and-composer.html
http://pitchfork.com/news/50746-daft-punk-cover-story-outtakes/
http://www.rollingstone.com/music/news/exclusive-daft-punk-reveal-secrets-of-new-album-20130413
http://www.spin.com/articles/daft-punk-random-access-memories-track-by-track-preview/
http://translate.google.com/translate?hl=en&sl=auto&tl=en&u=http%3A%2F%2Fobsession.nouvelobs.com%2Fmusique%2F20130418.OBS6224%2Frandom-access-memories-par-daft-punk.html

The Chart-Topper

http://en.wikipedia.org/wiki/Random_Access_Memories#cite_note-cz-109
http://www.mtv.com.au/news/daft-punk-land-biggest-debut-of-career-with-random-access-memories-ead47da4/
http://www.musicweek.com/news/read/daft-punk-s-get-lucky-track-surpasses-100m-streams-on-spotify/055824

http://www.nme.com/news/daft-punk/71973
http://www.sony.com/SCA/company-news/press-releases/sony-columbia-records/2013/daft-punks-random-access-memories-debuts-at-1-on-a.shtml
http://www.vh1.in/music/reviews/random-access-memories
http://www.youredm.com/2013/08/19/the-13-songs-of-the-summer-according-to-time/

The Phenomenon

http://www.cnn.com/2013/08/13/showbiz/tv/colbert-daft-punk-ew
http://consequenceofsound.net/2013/05/theres-now-a-daft-punk-racecar/
http://consequenceofsound.net/2013/07/daft-punk-action-figures-are-playing-at-my-house/
http://crfashionbook.com/post/58356929299/digital-love-a-tale-of-desire-starring-daft-punk
http://www.digitalspy.com/celebrity/news/a484803/daft-punk-join-up-with-lotus-f1-team-at-monaco-grand-prix-pictures.html
https://www.facebook.com/media/set/?set=a.570562746296228.1073741841.155435907808916&type=1
http://www.huffingtonpost.com/2013/08/15/daft-punk-milla-jovovich-photos_n_3763192.html
http://www.mirror.co.uk/news/uk-news/currys-job-applicants-forced-dance-off-2254279
http://www.mtv.com/news/articles/1713447/daft-punk-nile-rodgers-lose-yourself-to-dance.jhtml
http://newsfeed.time.com/2013/09/07/uk-retailer-apologizes-for-forcing-job-applicants-to-dance/
http://p-bandai.jp/tamashiiwebshouten/item-1000081552/
http://pitchfork.com/news/50868-watch-daft-punk-get-their-own-racecar-appear-in-ads/
http://pitchfork.com/news/51488-daft-punk-condoms-arent-official-durex-products/
http://pitchfork.com/news/51602-check-out-daft-punks-new-action-figures-vogue-spread/
http://sideshownetwork.tv/podcastsEpisode.cfm?podcastid=68&episodeID=2659
http://www.spin.com/articles/stephen-colbert-daft-punk-mtv-stunt/
http://www.sportspromedia.com/news/f1_lotus_announce_tie_up_with_columbia_records/
http://www.timeout.com/newyork/things-to-do/daft-punk-will-appear-on-the-colbert-report-tonight-video
http://translate.google.com/translate?hl=en&sl=auto&tl=en&u=http%3A%2F%2Fwww.telerama.fr%2Fmusique%2Fdaft-punk-l-interview-fleuve%2C97155.php
http://www.vibe.com/photo-gallery/vibe-summer-2013-cover-pharrell-and-daft-punk
http://www.vogue.com/magazine/article/what-to-wear-where-all-ages-show-karlie-kloss-and-daft-punk/#1

The Daft Punk Influence

http://www.billboard.com/articles/news/1049888/exclusive-live-album-to-chronicle-daft-punk-tour
http://doandroidsdance.com/features/the-10-best-daft-punk-samples-in-rap-tracks/
http://idolator.com/7457573/daft-punk-best-rap-songs-samples/5
http://www.nme.com/news/daft-punk/34231
http://www.whosampled.com/Daft-Punk/sampled/?sp=4

What's Next?

http://entertainment.time.com/2013/05/21/robocall-a-conversation-with-daft-punk%E2%80%A8%E2%80%A8-%E2%80%A8%E2%80%A8/

http://inserbia.info/news/2013/08/daft-punk-in-belgrade-in-2014/

http://music.cbc.ca/#/blogs/2013/5/How-Daft-Punks-2006-Coachella-show-revolutionized-live-electronic-music

http://www.mtv.com/news/articles/1710279/kanye-west-yeezus-daft-punk.jhtml

http://www.nme.com/news/daft-punk/72640

http://www.vibe.com/photo-gallery/vibe-summer-2013-cover-pharrell-and-daft-punk

IMAGE CREDITS

AUTHOR BIO

Voted one of the best Long Island authors for 2013, Dina Santorelli has been a freelance writer for more than fifteen years and has written frequently about travel, entertainment, lifestyle, weddings, and pop culture. Dina serves as the executive editor of *Salute* and *Family* magazines, for which she has interviewed many celebrities, including James Gandolfini, Tim McGraw, Bryan Adams, Ashanti, JR Martinez, David Cook, Angela Bassett, Mario Lopez, Gary Sinise, and Kevin Bacon, among others. She has collaborated on a variety of book projects and is a lecturer for Hofstra University's department of continuing education. Dina is currently working on a sequel to her debut novel, *Baby Grand,* a top-rated mystery and thriller on Amazon Kindle. For more information about Dina, visit her Web site at http://dinasantorelli.com.